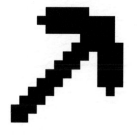

DEL REY
NEW YORK

Stay safe online. Any website addresses listed in this book are correct at the time of
going to print. However, Del Rey is not responsible for content hosted by third parties.
Please be aware that online content can be subject to change and websites can contain
content that is unsuitable for children. We advise that all children are supervised when
using the Internet. This publisher does not have any control over and does not assume
any responsibility for author or third-party websites or their content.

ONLINE SAFETY FOR YOUNGER FANS
Spending time online is great fun! Here are a few simple rules to help younger fans stay
safe and keep the Internet a great place to spend time:
- Never give out your real name—don't use it as your username.
- Never give out any of your personal details.
- Never tell anybody which school you go to or how old you are.
- Never tell anybody your password except a parent or a guardian.
- Be aware that you must be 13 or over to create an account on many sites. Always check
the site policy and ask a parent or guardian for permission before registering.
- Always tell a parent or guardian if something is worrying you.

Published in the United States by Del Rey, an imprint of Random House,
a division of Penguin Random House LLC, New York.

DEL REY and the HOUSE colophon are registered trademarks of Penguin Random House LLC.

Published in hardcover in the United Kingdom by Egmont UK Limited.

ISBN 978-0-593-15813-5
Ebook ISBN 978-0-593-15814-2

Printed in China on acid-free paper by C & C Offset

Written by Stephanie Milton

Illustrations by Ryan Marsh

randomhousebooks.com

2 4 6 8 9 7 5 3 1

First US Edition

Design by Richie Hull, Paul Lang and John Stuckey

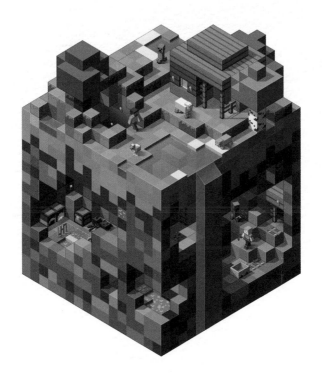

GUIDE TO:
⤤SURVIVAL

CONTENTS

1. THE MINECRAFT LANDSCAPE

2. MOBS

3. SURVIVAL

INTRODUCTION

Welcome to the official *Guide to Survival*! There's something very special about starting a new game of Minecraft's Survival mode. A fresh, never-before-explored Overworld lies all around, and it's up to you to build the life you want to lead within it.

You know it'll take work. A lot of knowledge. Maybe a little luck, too. You'll go on adventures, and come across amazing sights and priceless treasures. It won't be long until you'll feel that the world is yours. But a little extra know-how is always helpful! We've packed this guide with hints and tips gathered from years of experience. You'll learn about the different biomes waiting to be discovered and what you might find in each one, the mobs you'll encounter on your journey, and some of the vital items you'll need to survive and thrive.

Happy Minecrafting!

ALEX WILTSHIRE
THE MOJANG TEAM

THE TECHNICAL STUFF

Before you start your first game there are some decisions to make about how you'd like to play. This page will help you decide whether you'd like to venture out alone or as part of a group, and which game mode is right for you.

WHICH DEVICE?

You can play Minecraft on lots of different devices. Bedrock Edition is the version of the game you play on Windows 10, Xbox One, Nintendo Switch, mobile devices, Gear VR and Fire TV. People across all these devices can play together. You can also play Minecraft on PC or Mac (Java Edition), on PlayStation, Xbox 360, Wii U and Nintendo 3DS. This book covers Bedrock Edition.

SINGLE PLAYER OR MULTIPLAYER?

Once you've chosen a device, you can decide what kind of adventure you want to have, whether that's alone or with friends.

Single player is the original, default mode for Minecraft. This mode is for you if you prefer to take on the challenges of Minecraft alone rather than in a team.

Choose multiplayer if you want to share your adventure with friends on the same network. One person will need to set up a LAN (local area network) game for the others to join.

GAME MODE

Finally, there are several different game modes to choose from, offering various degrees of difficulty.

SURVIVAL
Choose Survival mode and you'll have loads of fun fighting hostile monsters and collecting materials to help you stay alive. You'll need to eat, and you'll gain experience and levels as you play.

CREATIVE
In Creative mode, you're free from hostile mobs, you can fly around and destroy blocks instantly. You'll also have a full inventory of materials with which to build amazing structures.

HARDCORE
If you choose Hardcore mode, the difficulty will be locked on hard and you'll only get one life. If you die, it really will be game over – your world will be deleted and you'll have to start again.

PEACEFUL
You can also choose a peaceful option in Survival mode. You'll still collect materials and craft in order to survive, but without the hostile mobs. And your health will regenerate, too.

THIS IS YOU

Now you've decided how you want to play, you can open Minecraft. But before you hit "play" and start your first game, you'll need to choose the character that you'll be playing as.

CHOOSING YOUR CHARACTER

Click on the clothes hanger icon toward the bottom of the screen. There are 2 skins (character designs) for you to choose from: Steve and Alex. Select the character you'd like to play as, then press "confirm." Now you're ready to play!

STEVE

ALEX

HEADS-UP DISPLAY

As you play, some important information about your character will be displayed on screen. This information is called your heads-up display (or HUD). Let's take a look at what everything means.

CROSSHAIRS
This little cross helps you to aim at blocks you want to mine or at monsters you want to hit. It shows the exact point where you will use the tool or item you have in your hand.

HEALTH BAR
Your health bar shows how much life you have left. It's made up of 10 hearts – each heart is worth 2 health points, so you have a total of 20 health points. You lose health points if you don't eat, and if you take damage (e.g. when a monster attacks you). Always keep your health bar as full as you can.

HUNGER BAR
Your hunger bar is very important, too – it affects your health bar. It's made up of 10 drumsticks. You have a total of 20 hunger points, so each drumstick is worth 2 hunger points. You need to keep it topped up or you will start to lose health points.

EXPERIENCE
This bar shows you how much experience you've earned so far. You can earn experience points by mining, smelting ores and defeating mobs. Green balls called experience orbs will appear and you will automatically collect them if you're standing close enough. Experience adds up to levels.

HOTBAR
These 9 slots are great for storing the items you use most often. There's also a single slot to the left of the hotbar called the off-hand slot. If the hotbar slot you currently have selected is empty and you hit the "use item" button, you will use the item in your off-hand slot.

INVENTORY

When you play in Survival, Hardcore or Peaceful mode you'll collect lots of useful blocks and items, which you'll need to store and manage in your inventory. You can open your inventory at any time while you're playing. Let's take a look at the inventory in more detail.

ARMOR SLOTS
See page 89 for instructions on how to craft and equip armor.

CRAFTING GRID
Drag materials into the crafting grid to craft simple items such as wood planks and torches.

OUTPUT SQUARE
Your newly crafted item will appear in your output square, ready to put in your inventory.

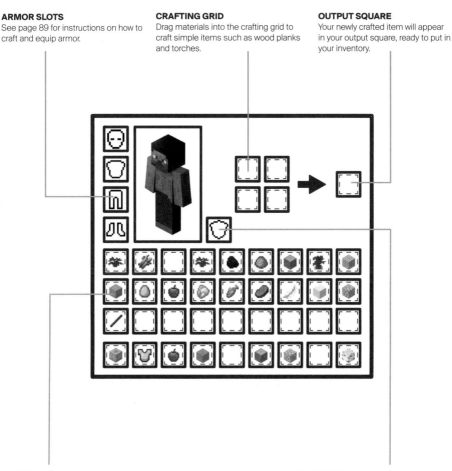

ITEM SLOTS
There are 27 item slots available. Many blocks and items can be stacked together, up to a maximum of 64. Some items, like eggs and buckets, can only be stacked up to a maximum of 16. Items like tools cannot be stacked at all. Hover over any item in your inventory and its name will appear.

OFF-HAND SLOT
Your off-hand slot can be equipped to hold a second item, which will enable you to dual-wield. You will automatically use the item in your off-hand slot when there is no item in your main slot. You can't use weapons when they're in your off-hand slot, but it's ideal for items like arrows, food or torches.

9

KEY

Throughout this book you'll see symbols that represent different items, values or properties – they cover everything from causes of damage to mob drops. Refer back to this page when you spot them to check what they mean.

GENERAL

MOJANG STUFF

This super-exclusive info has come directly from the developers at Mojang.

∞

Indicates that this item is an unlimited drop while the mob in question is alive.

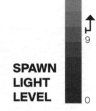

15

9

0

SPAWN LIGHT LEVEL

Indicates the light level at which a mob spawns. In this example, the mob spawns at a light level of 9 or higher.

Mob does not die when the sun rises.

HOSTILITY

Indicates the hostility level of a mob – yellow is passive, orange is neutral and red is hostile.

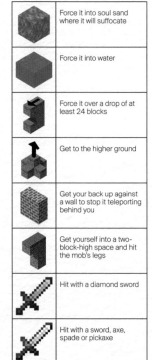
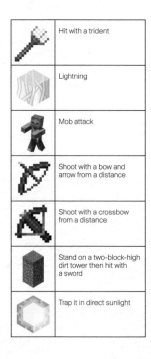

Blow it up with TNT		Force it into soul sand where it will suffocate		Hit with a trident	
Disable mob spawner with 5 torches		Force it into water		Lightning	
Drink milk to neutralize poison effects		Force it over a drop of at least 24 blocks		Mob attack	
Enemy player attack		Get to the higher ground		Shoot with a bow and arrow from a distance	
Falling anvil		Get your back up against a wall to stop it teleporting behind you		Shoot with a crossbow from a distance	
Fire		Get yourself into a two-block-high space and hit the mob's legs		Stand on a two-block-high dirt tower then hit with a sword	
Force it into cacti		Hit with a diamond sword		Trap it in direct sunlight	
Force it into lava		Hit with a sword, axe, spade or pickaxe			

ITEMS, BLOCKS AND EFFECTS

	Armor		Enchanted book		Music disc		Raw rabbit
	Arrow		Ender pearl		Mushroom (brown)		Raw salmon
	Bamboo		Experience point		Mushroom (red)		Redstone
	Bone		Feather		Naturally spawned equipment		Rotten flesh
	Bow		Fireball, fire charge or ender acid ball		Paper		Saddle
	Bowl		Glass bottle		Phantom membrane		Scute
	Carpet		Glowstone dust		Picked-up equipment		Seagrass
	Carrot		Gold ingot		Potato		Skeleton head
	Chest		Golden nugget		Potion of invisibility		Slimeball
	Clownfish		Gunpowder		Prismarine crystal		Spider eye
	Cooked chicken		Horse armor		Prismarine shard		Steak
	Cooked cod		Illager banner		Pufferfish		Stick
	Cooked mutton		Ink sac		Rabbit hide		String
	Cooked porkchop		Iron axe		Rabbit's foot		Sugar
	Cooked rabbit		Iron ingot		Raw beef		Totem of undying
	Cooked salmon		Iron shovel		Raw chicken		Trident
	Creeper head		Lead		Raw cod		Wet sponge
	Crossbow		Leather		Raw mutton		Wool
	Egg		Milk bucket		Raw porkchop		Zombie head
	Emerald						

BEFORE YOU SPAWN

This guide assumes you are playing alone in Survival mode. Before you start your first game (and "spawn" into the world you've created), there are a few things to understand about the mysterious world of Minecraft.

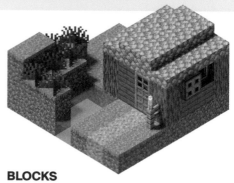

WORLD SEED

This is the string of numbers or characters that generates every Minecraft world and determines what it will look like. People often share the best seeds online. The world seed is set automatically, but you can set it manually if there's a particular seed you'd like to try – go to "create new world" then "more world options" to enter the seed.

BLOCKS

The Minecraft landscape is made of naturally generated blocks, but you can also craft blocks yourself. Blocks can be placed on top of other blocks and used for building. Some are opaque, others transparent, and they can be liquid or solid. Many blocks also have a function, e.g. torches provide a light source and cake restores food points.

ITEMS

Items can't be placed in the Minecraft world but can be held and dropped for other players to pick up. They generally have a function, e.g. tools, and can often be combined with other items to craft blocks, e.g. gunpowder.

MOBS

Mob is short for "mobile" and refers to all living, moving creatures. Mobs can be passive, neutral or hostile. Some mobs are tameable, and two are categorized as utility mobs since they can help to defend you.

BREAKING BLOCKS

You need to break blocks to collect them. Some, e.g. wood, can be broken by hand or with a tool. Other blocks can only be broken with a specific tool, such as a pickaxe. Some tools allow you to break certain blocks more quickly – for example, a spade breaks sand, grass and gravel the fastest.

HEALTH POINTS AND DEATH

As we know, in Survival mode your health points decrease if you take damage and if you don't eat. If you lose all 20 health points, you will find yourself back at the respawn screen. The contents of your inventory will be dropped at the site of your demise – if you're quick you can run back and pick everything up.

DAY AND NIGHT CYCLE

A complete day/night cycle lasts 20 minutes – 10 minutes of day followed by 10 minutes of night. The sun and moon rise and fall in the sky, so check their position to give you an idea of how much day or night is left.

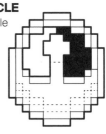

COORDINATES

Coordinates are numbers that tell you where you are. The x axis is your distance east or west from your spawn point, the z axis is your distance north or south and the y axis shows how high or low you are. Check your coordinates on a PC or Mac by pressing F3, or by consulting a map item when playing on a console.

LEVELS AND EXPERIENCE

Experience points are earned through mining, defeating mobs and players, using furnaces and breeding animals. Experience orbs will appear and you'll automatically collect them if you're standing close enough. Gain enough points to increase your level, or use them to make enchanted tools, weapons and armor with new abilities.

1

THE MINECRAFT LANDSCAPE

This section is all about the physical landscape of your Minecraft world. You'll learn about the different biomes you might spawn in and discover the pros and cons of settling in each. You'll also learn where to search for fascinating naturally generated structures and valuable loot that will help you on your journey.

BIOMES

BADLANDS

Rare badlands biomes are largely composed of terracotta and red sand. There are very few trees and no passive mobs to provide meat, so avoid this biome when you first spawn. Gold ore generates at all levels here.

BADLANDS VARIANTS

These variants contain flat, tree-covered areas and terracotta spikes respectively.

PLATEAU

ERODED BADLANDS

ABANDONED MINE SHAFT

Abandoned mine shafts generate at surface level, giving you access to rare ores.

DARK FOREST

Dark forest biomes have a dense covering of dark oak trees and huge mushrooms that block out most of the sunlight.

HOSTILE MOBS

Hostile mobs often spawn during the day due to the low light level, so this is not a biome for beginners to settle in.

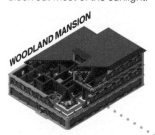

WOODLAND MANSION

These rare structures are packed with loot, but crawling with dangerous mobs.

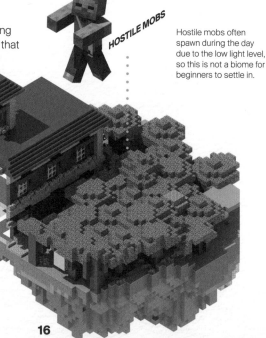

DESERT

Desert biomes are barren and inhospitable. Most passive mobs don't spawn here, and rain doesn't fall, so finding and growing food is difficult. Visit deserts to collect resources but build your base in a more hospitable biome.

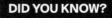
DID YOU KNOW?

Look out for fossils when mining in desert biomes – they generate 15-24 blocks below the surface and are made of bone blocks. It's thought they are the remains of giant, extinct creatures...

DESERT WELL

Desert wells can sometimes be found, too – these are largely decorative but can also be used as a water source.

DESERT TEMPLE

Desert temples and villages are common features. Both are a great source of materials and also contain loot chests in which you can find more valuable items and blocks.

CACTUS

There are no trees to provide wood – the surface is covered with sand, dead bushes and cacti.

FOREST

Forests are an ideal spawn point, as they provide lots of wood for crafting. The surface is covered with oak trees.

FOREST VARIANTS

Flower forests have fewer trees but an abundance of colorful flowers.

BIRCH FOREST

FLOWER FOREST

The birch forest variant contains only birch trees.

HOSTILE MOBS

Hostile mobs can hide in the shade under the trees and surprise you during the day.

JUNGLE

Jungles are difficult to travel across and build in due to the dense covering of trees. Hostile mobs can spawn in the daytime as the tree canopy blocks out a lot of sunlight, so avoid settling here when you first spawn. This is the only biome in which you can find melons and cocoa.

JUNGLE VARIANT

Bamboo jungles have fewer trees but lots of bamboo. Pandas spawn here – see page 42 for more info.

BAMBOO JUNGLE

Ocelots and parrots spawn exclusively in jungles. See pages 38 and 43 for more info.

JUNGLE TEMPLE

Jungle temples contain trapped loot chests – see page 27 for more info.

PASSIVE MOBS

MOUNTAINS

Mountains are impressive to look at, but building is difficult due to the lack of flat ground, and exploring is dangerous as you can fall from the cliffs.

EMERALD ORE

Emerald ore only generates in mountains, so it's a good biome for mining.

LLAMA

Llamas spawn in herds in the mountains – see page 41 for more info.

MUSHROOM FIELDS

The rare mushroom fields biome can be found in the middle of the ocean. It's a mixture of hills and plains, covered in mycelium. Mushroom fields are one of only two biomes in which huge mushrooms grow naturally. The biome is a safe refuge for beginners, but trees don't grow here so you'll need to move on if you want to craft useful items.

Mooshrooms are the only mob that spawns here – there are no hostile mobs.

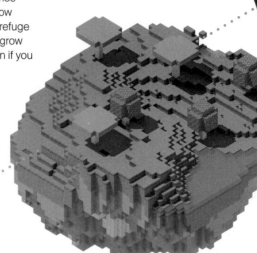

MOOSHROOM

MYCELIUM

Mycelium is a block on which mushrooms and huge mushrooms grow at any light level.

OCEAN

There are four kinds of ocean biome: warm, lukewarm, cold and frozen. They're teeming with life – you'll meet everything from friendly dolphins to deadly drowned mobs. There are plenty of fish to provide food, too. They're also laden with loot, so keep an eye out for underwater ruins and shipwrecks.

OCEAN MONUMENT

Treasure-laden monuments generate in deep areas of ocean and are patrolled by dangerous guardians and elder guardians.

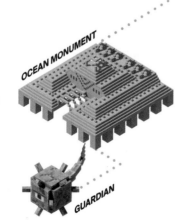

GUARDIAN

PLAINS

Plains are flat and grassy, with only a sparse covering of trees. Villages are commonly found here, and they're one of only a few biomes in which horses spawn naturally. They're relatively easy to build in, so they're great for beginners and for settling long-term.

PASSIVE MOBS

Plains are a great source of food due to the abundance of passive mobs.

PLAINS VARIANT

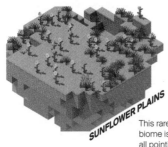

SUNFLOWER PLAINS

This rare variant of the plains biome is covered in sunflowers, all pointing east to help you get your bearings.

SAVANNA

Savannas are arid, flat biomes covered with dry grass and acacia trees. Farming can be difficult due to the lack of water. Horses and llamas spawn frequently in savannas.

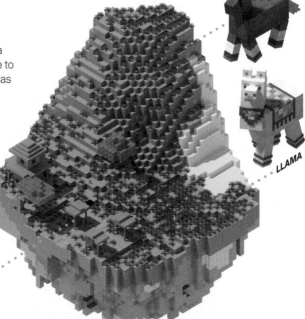

HORSE

LLAMA

VILLAGE

Villages are common in savannas, so they're a good biome in which to gather resources.

SNOWY TUNDRA

Snowy tundras are flat, snowy biomes in which all exposed water sources have frozen to ice. Sugar cane is often found here, but farming is difficult since water freezes. There aren't many trees, so it's not ideal for beginners.

SNOWY TUNDRA VARIANT

In this variant biome you'll find large spikes of ice. Some can reach over 50 blocks in height.

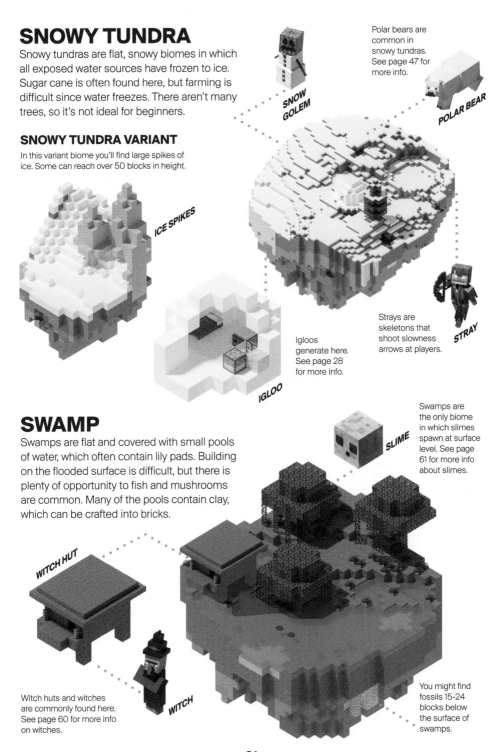

Polar bears are common in snowy tundras. See page 47 for more info.

SNOW GOLEM

POLAR BEAR

ICE SPIKES

Igloos generate here. See page 28 for more info.

Strays are skeletons that shoot slowness arrows at players.

STRAY

IGLOO

SWAMP

Swamps are flat and covered with small pools of water, which often contain lily pads. Building on the flooded surface is difficult, but there is plenty of opportunity to fish and mushrooms are common. Many of the pools contain clay, which can be crafted into bricks.

Swamps are the only biome in which slimes spawn at surface level. See page 61 for more info about slimes.

SLIME

WITCH HUT

Witch huts and witches are commonly found here. See page 60 for more info on witches.

WITCH

You might find fossils 15-24 blocks below the surface of swamps.

TAIGA

Taiga biomes are a great source of wood due to the abundance of spruce trees, making them a good starting point for beginners. You'll find wolves, rabbits and foxes here, as well as villages.

TAIGA VARIANT

This sub-biome is covered in a type of dirt called podzol and has giant trees.

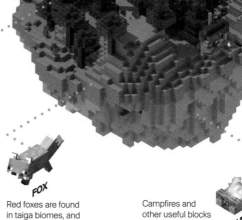

GIANT TREE TAIGA

FOX

Red foxes are found in taiga biomes, and white foxes appear in the snowy taiga variant.

Campfires and other useful blocks can be found in taiga villages.

CAMPFIRE

THE NETHER

You'll never spawn here, but more advanced players will want to visit the Nether – a hellish dimension filled with new and terrifying hostile mobs. The Nether is a great source of unique materials such as glowstone, which can be used as a light source, and Nether quartz, which can be turned into quartz for building.

Nether mobs drop an array of useful items, many of which are needed for potions.

HOSTILE MOBS

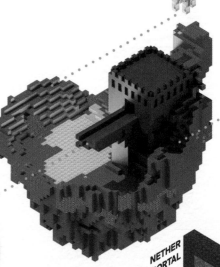

NETHER FORTRESS

Nether fortresses are the only naturally generated structure in the Nether. They contain several useful materials including Nether wart, which you'll need for potions.

NETHER PORTAL

The Nether is accessed via a portal that you'll build from obsidian then set alight to activate.

THE END

The End is composed of several islands floating in the Void. Only the most advanced players dare venture there ...

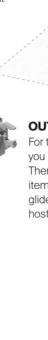

ENDER DRAGON

MAIN ISLAND

The main island is accessed via an End portal in a stronghold in the Overworld – see page 30 for more info. If you want to get out of there alive and visit the outer islands, you'll need to defeat the ultimate boss mob – the ender dragon.

OUTER ISLANDS

For those skillful enough to defeat the dragon, you must then find a way to the outer islands. There you'll find unique blocks, as well as rare items such as elytra (wings that allow you to glide), a decorative dragon head and a new hostile mob – the shulker.

MOJANG STUFF

As in the Nether, sleeping in a bed in the End will cause it to explode. One speedrun challenge in Hardcore mode is to find a way of placing beds during the climactic battle so that you are partly shielded from the explosion, but inflict maximum damage to the dragon as it swoops in. Timing is everything!

NATURALLY GENERATED STRUCTURES

If you know where to look, you'll find naturally generated structures all around you. These structures contain valuable materials and sometimes loot chests, too, but they're dangerous and often contain traps. Proceed with caution.

ABANDONED MINE SHAFT

Usually found underground, abandoned mine shafts are an excellent place to mine for ores.

Beware of cave spider spawners, which are surrounded by a heavy layer of cobwebs. Cave spiders are venomous and can soon overpower you in the narrow corridors.

Watch out for lava streams and pools, which are common underground.

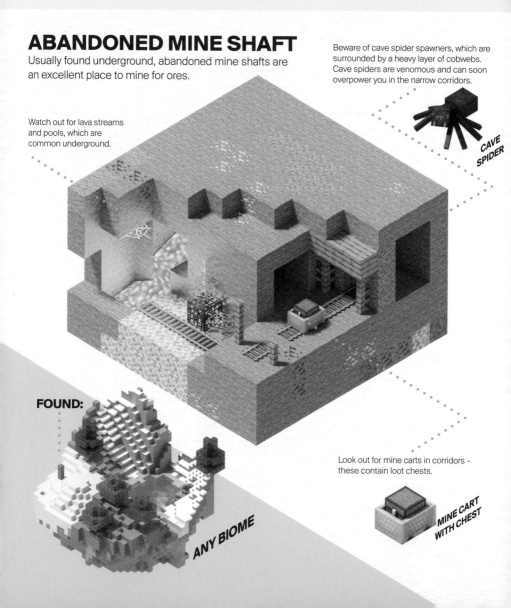

CAVE SPIDER

FOUND:

ANY BIOME

Look out for mine carts in corridors – these contain loot chests.

MINE CART WITH CHEST

DESERT TEMPLE

Desert temples are found in desert biomes. They are constructed from various sandstone blocks, with decorative blocks of orange and blue terracotta. You can mine these blocks for use in your own constructions.

Desert temples may be partially buried in sand and can be difficult to spot. Look out for sandstone and orange terracotta, or a tower protruding from the landscape.

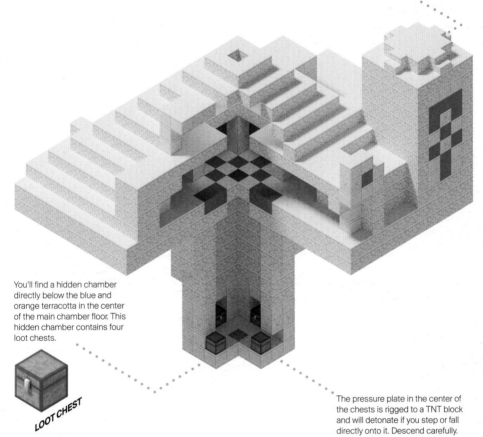

You'll find a hidden chamber directly below the blue and orange terracotta in the center of the main chamber floor. This hidden chamber contains four loot chests.

The pressure plate in the center of the chests is rigged to a TNT block and will detonate if you step or fall directly onto it. Descend carefully.

LOOT CHEST

TNT

FOUND:

DESERT

DUNGEON

Dungeons are small rooms built out of mossy cobblestone and cobblestone. They usually generate underground, and you can wander into them fairly easily. Keep an eye out for mossy cobblestone or flames flickering in the darkness when mining.

You'll find a zombie, skeleton or spider spawner in the center of the dungeon, which you can disable by placing torches around and on top of it. Alternatively, you could use the spawner for combat practice.

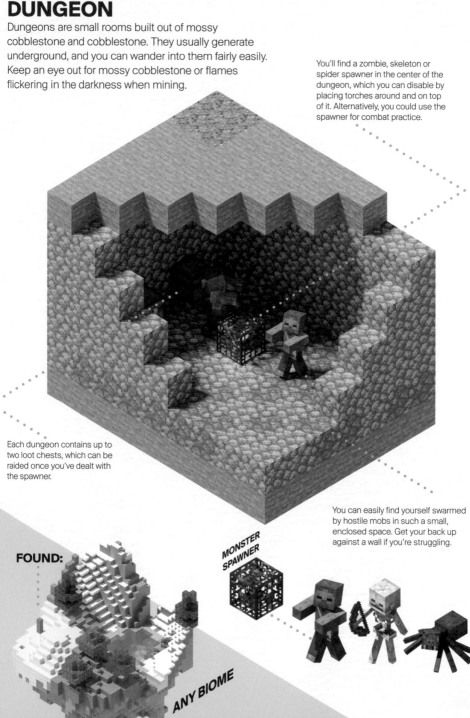

Each dungeon contains up to two loot chests, which can be raided once you've dealt with the spawner.

You can easily find yourself swarmed by hostile mobs in such a small, enclosed space. Get your back up against a wall if you're struggling.

FOUND:

MONSTER SPAWNER

ANY BIOME

JUNGLE TEMPLE

Built from cobblestone, mossy cobblestone and chiselled stone bricks, mysterious jungle temples have three floors and can be accessed via an entrance at ground level.

Down in the basement you'll find three levers. When pulled in the right order they'll reveal a secret chamber back on the ground floor which contains a loot chest.

The top floor is empty but can be mined for mossy cobblestone.

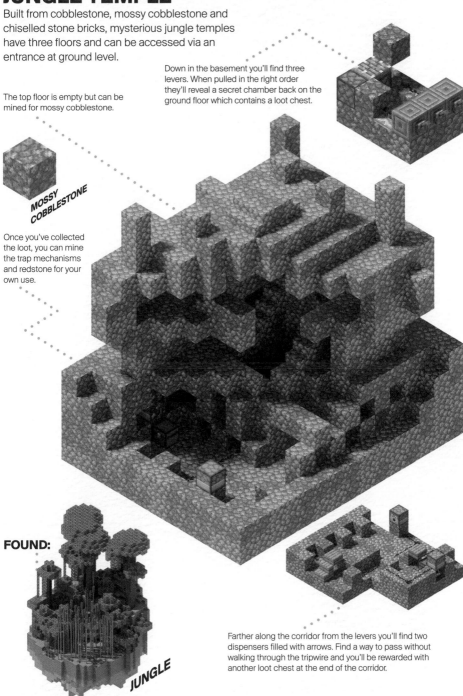

MOSSY COBBLESTONE

Once you've collected the loot, you can mine the trap mechanisms and redstone for your own use.

FOUND:

JUNGLE

Farther along the corridor from the levers you'll find two dispensers filled with arrows. Find a way to pass without walking through the tripwire and you'll be rewarded with another loot chest at the end of the corridor.

IGLOO

Igloos are small structures composed of snow blocks. They make useful emergency shelters.

Inside you'll find carpet, a bed, a crafting table and a furnace.

Half of igloos also contain a basement, accessed via a trapdoor under the carpet.

The basement contains a brewing stand, a loot chest, a cauldron and two cells imprisoning a villager and a zombie villager. Mine the brewing stand and cauldron with a pickaxe – you'll need them to brew potions.

FOUND:

SNOWY TUNDRA / COLD TAIGA

Watch out for silverfish in the basement – some of the wall blocks are actually monster eggs.

VILLAGE

Home to your friendly local villagers, villages contain a variety of structures with different functions, from houses and farms to a blacksmith and libraries.

Watch out for zombie villagers, especially in small villages with no iron golem.

ZOMBIE VILLAGER

Villagers spawn in the building relating to their profession. During the day, they leave their buildings and wander around the village.

VILLAGER

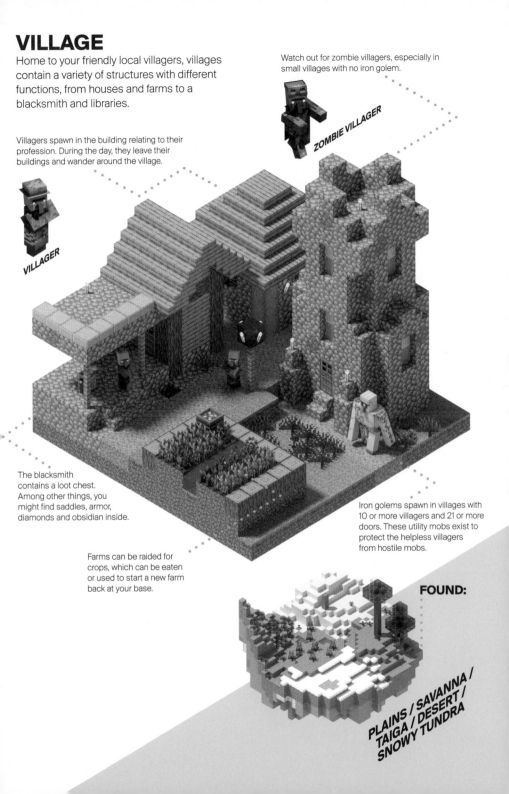

The blacksmith contains a loot chest. Among other things, you might find saddles, armor, diamonds and obsidian inside.

Iron golems spawn in villages with 10 or more villagers and 21 or more doors. These utility mobs exist to protect the helpless villagers from hostile mobs.

Farms can be raided for crops, which can be eaten or used to start a new farm back at your base.

FOUND:

PLAINS / SAVANNA / TAIGA / DESERT / SNOWY TUNDRA

STRONGHOLD

Strongholds are found underground, and sometimes underwater. You'll need to find a stronghold if you want to visit the End.

Throw eyes of ender to locate your nearest stronghold. Each eye will travel a short distance in the right direction. When they stop traveling and fall onto the same spot, dig down to find the stronghold.

Strongholds vary in size. They are composed of several rooms, connected by a maze of corridors and staircases. It's easy to get lost in large strongholds as you search for the End portal room.

Look out for loot chests as you explore. These may contain everything from enchanted books to diamond horse armor.

FOUND:

ANY BIOME

The End portal room contains an incomplete End portal and a silverfish spawner. You'll need to fill the empty End portal frames with eyes of ender to activate it, then jump through to be transported to the End.

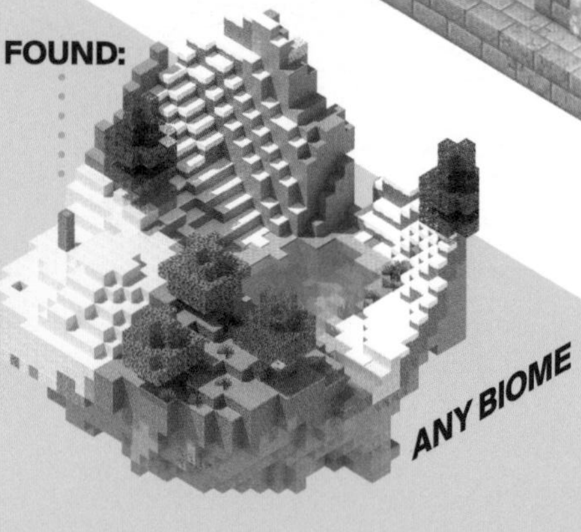

PILLAGER OUTPOST

Pillager outposts generate around 100-150 blocks away from villages. They're home to hostile pillagers who like to carry out raids on the villages.

IRON GOLEM

Iron golems can be found in cages around some towers.

The main structure looks like a watchtower.

You'll find a loot chest in the watchtower. This could contain everything from carrots to an enchanted book.

There will usually be other structures around the tower.

FOUND:

PLAINS / SAVANNA / TAIGA / DESERT / SNOWY TUNDRA

WOODLAND MANSION

Woodland mansions are a rare sight in dark forest biomes. Built from wood and cobblestone, they have several floors, many rooms and offer an abundance of useful resources. Sound too good to be true? Unfortunately they're also home to some of Minecraft's most dangerous mobs.

In addition to the usual hostile mobs, vindicator, evoker and vex mobs spawn inside the mansion. These boss-like mobs are highly dangerous and only skilled players should attempt to take them on. See pages 62-63 to learn more.

VEX

VINDICATOR   EVOKER

You may find several farming areas on the ground floor, including a tree farm, mushroom farm and pumpkin and melon patches.

FOUND:

DARK FOREST

DID YOU KNOW? ↗

Explorer maps are handy items that help you track down woodland mansions – see page 45 to learn how to get your hands on one.

Several rooms have a more homely feel – dining rooms contain tables, flower pots and bookshelves, and you might find many bedrooms, too.

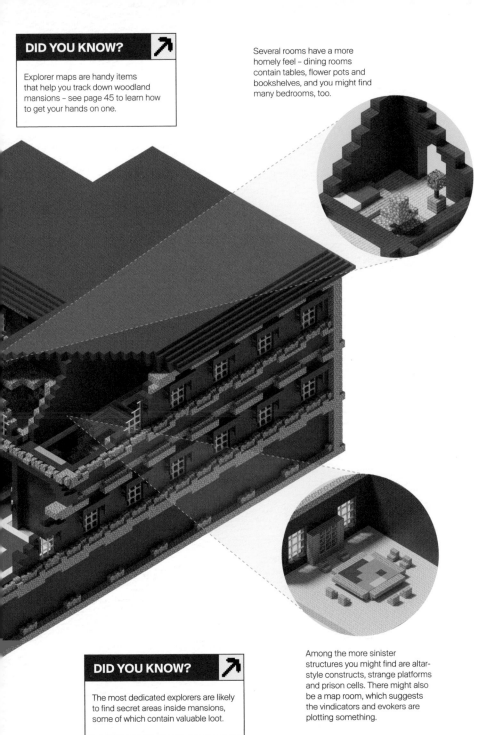

DID YOU KNOW? ↗

The most dedicated explorers are likely to find secret areas inside mansions, some of which contain valuable loot.

Among the more sinister structures you might find are altar-style constructs, strange platforms and prison cells. There might also be a map room, which suggests the vindicators and evokers are plotting something.

2

MOBS

You're not alone in this mysterious new world. In this section, you'll discover the differences between passive, neutral and hostile mobs. You'll learn where to find them, how to defend yourself from neutral and hostile mob attacks and, most importantly, what each mob drops when defeated.

PASSIVE MOBS

As you explore the Overworld, you'll come across a variety of passive mobs that can easily be defeated with a tool or weapon. Most drop useful items, including meat, which will be cooked if they are defeated when on fire.

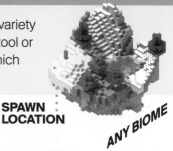

SPAWN LOCATION

ANY BIOME

CHICKEN

BEHAVIOR
Chickens spawn in grassy areas. They wander around, clucking and laying eggs every 5-10 minutes.

SPECIAL SKILLS
When falling, chickens slow their descent by flapping their wings so they don't take damage.

DROPS WHEN ALIVE

∞

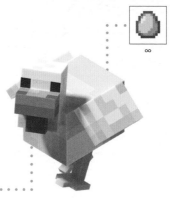

DROPS WHEN DEFEATED

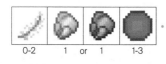

| 0-2 | 1 | or | 1 | 1-3 |

15

↑⌐
9

SPAWN LIGHT LEVEL

0

BAT

BEHAVIOR
Bats spawn in caves across the Overworld. They hang upside-down when idle, but otherwise can be seen flying around erratically.

SPECIAL SKILLS
Bats are the only passive mob that spawns in the dark and that can fly.

DROPS WHEN DEFEATED

0

MOJANG STUFF

The high-pitched squeak the bat makes was toned down several times after players said it hurt their ears.

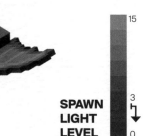

15

3
⌐↓

SPAWN LIGHT LEVEL

0

36

PIG

BEHAVIOR
Pigs roam the Overworld in groups of 3-4, oinking randomly. They will follow any player that is within 5 blocks of them and is holding a carrot, a carrot on a stick, a potato or beetroot.

See page 75 for a fishing rod recipe. Carrots can be found in village farms and can be dropped by zombies.

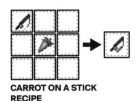

CARROT ON A STICK RECIPE

SPECIAL SKILLS
Pigs can be ridden, although they aren't very fast. You'll need to saddle them first, then lead them around using a carrot on a stick. They will eat the carrot over time, so you'll need to keep an eye on its durability bar. Saddles can be found in naturally generated chests. A saddled pig will drop its saddle upon death.

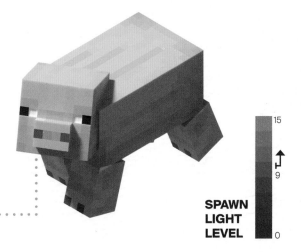

DROPS WHEN DEFEATED

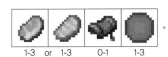

| 1-3 | or | 1-3 | 0-1 | 1-3 |

SPAWN LIGHT LEVEL

SHEEP

BEHAVIOR
Sheep wander around, bleating occasionally and eating grass blocks.

DROPS WHEN ALIVE

1-3

SPECIAL SKILLS
Sheep drop 1 wool when they die, but 1-3 wool if you shear them while they're alive. The wool will grow back after shearing. You can also dye a sheep before you shear it to permanently change the wool's color. Dyes can be crafted from flowers, lapis lazuli, cocoa beans and ink sacs, among other items.

DROPS WHEN DEFEATED

| 1 | 1-2 | or | 1-2 | 1-3 |

SPAWN LIGHT LEVEL

OCELOT

BEHAVIOR
Ocelots creep through jungles, occasionally attacking chickens. They avoid players and hostile mobs.

SPECIAL SKILLS
Ocelots scare creepers away and are immune to fall damage. They can be bred by feeding them raw fish. Stand within 10 blocks of an ocelot, then wait for it to enter begging mode – it will walk right up to you and look at you. Don't make any sudden movements or you'll scare it off. Feed 2 ocelots raw fish and they will make a baby ocelot. Once you've fed an ocelot, it will trust you and stop running away.

SPAWN LOCATION

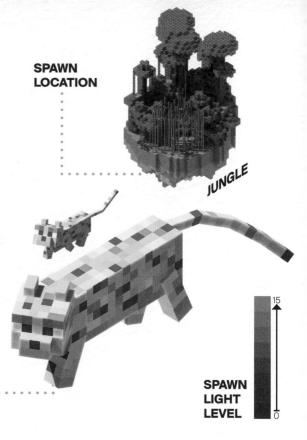

JUNGLE

DROPS WHEN DEFEATED

1-3

15

SPAWN LIGHT LEVEL

0

RABBIT

BEHAVIOR
Rabbits hop around, avoiding players, hostile mobs and wolves. They seek out and eat mature carrot crops.

SPECIAL SKILLS
Rabbits will approach you if you're within 8 blocks and are holding carrots or dandelions. They will go over cliffs to reach carrots, but not through lava.

DROPS WHEN DEFEATED

| 0-1 | 0-1 | or | 0-1 | 0-1 | 1-3 |

15

7

SPAWN LIGHT LEVEL

0

SQUID

BEHAVIOR
Squid move through water using their tentacles. If attacked, they try to swim away. They suffocate if not in water.

SPECIAL SKILLS
Squid can swim against a current. They also have an impressive set of teeth, although they are harmless.

DROPS WHEN DEFEATED

1-3	1-3

SPAWN LOCATION

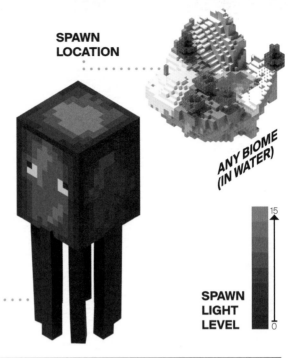

ANY BIOME (IN WATER)

SPAWN LIGHT LEVEL

15

0

HORSE

BEHAVIOR
Horses roam in herds of 2-6. They can have 1 of 35 different color and marking combinations. Donkeys are a smaller variant of horse. If a horse breeds with a donkey they will produce a mule.

SPECIAL SKILLS
Horses are one of the fastest methods of transport, but they need to be tamed first. Tame a horse by mounting it repeatedly until it stops throwing you off, then saddle it so it can be ridden. Saddles can be found in naturally generated chests. Donkeys and mules can also be equipped with chests and used to transport items. When defeated, horses will drop any equipment they have, and donkeys and mules will drop their chest, if equipped, plus its contents.

DROPS WHEN DEFEATED

0-2	0-1	0-1	0-1	1-3

SPAWN LOCATION

SAVANNA/ PLAINS

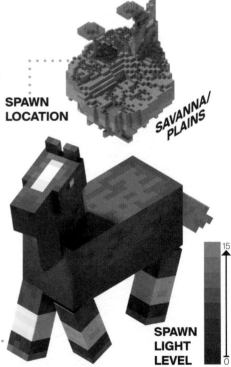

SPAWN LIGHT LEVEL

15

0

COW

BEHAVIOR
Cows travel in groups and can be heard mooing from quite some distance.

SPECIAL SKILLS
Cows can be milked by using a bucket on them. See page 73 for a bucket recipe. They also follow you if you're holding wheat within 10 blocks of them. They may drop leather when defeated, which can be used in several crafting recipes, and will drop meat, which will be cooked if they were killed by fire.

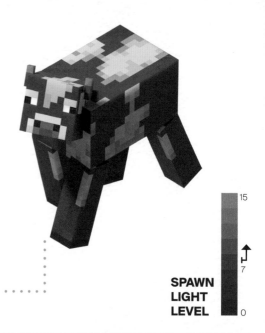

DROPS WHEN DEFEATED

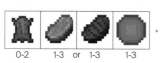

| 0-2 | 1-3 | or | 1-3 | 1-3 |

SPAWN LIGHT LEVEL

15

7

0

MOOSHROOM

BEHAVIOR
Mooshrooms can only be found in mushroom fields biomes. They wander around in herds of 4-8, avoiding danger such as cliffs and lava.

SPAWN LOCATION
MUSHROOM FIELDS

SPECIAL SKILLS
Mooshrooms can be milked by using a bucket on them. They can also be milked with a bowl to produce mushroom stew, and sheared for 5 mushrooms (red or brown depending on the type of mooshroom), which will turn them into regular cows. In all other respects they are very similar to cows – they may drop leather when defeated, and will drop 1-3 pieces of meat, which will be cooked if they were killed by fire.

DROPS WHEN ALIVE

0-5

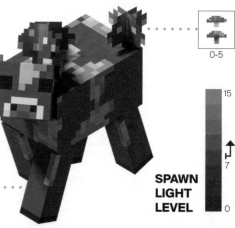

DROPS WHEN DEFEATED

| 0-2 | 1-3 | or | 1-3 | 1-3 |

SPAWN LIGHT LEVEL

15

7

0

LLAMA

BEHAVIOR

Llamas like to stay together in herds. If one llama is led by a player, nearby llamas will follow, forming a caravan. They are hostile toward wolves and will spit at them, dealing a small amount of damage. They will also spit at any player who attacks them.

SPECIAL SKILLS

Tame a llama by riding it a few times with an empty hand, until it stops throwing you off. Once tamed, you can equip a llama with a chest, and with a carpet to change the appearance of its saddle. It will drop any equipped items when defeated.

SAVANNA

MOUNTAINS

DROPS WHEN DEFEATED

| 0-2 | 0-1 | 0-1 | 1-3 |

DID YOU KNOW?

Each llama has its own unique strength rating that determines how many items it can carry. They're all equally adorable, however.

**SPAWN
LIGHT
LEVEL**

15

7

0

CAT

BEHAVIOR

These tameable mobs can be found wandering around villages as strays. They will have 1 of 11 different skins. Black cats can also spawn in witch huts in swamps.

SPECIAL SKILLS

Stray cats can be tamed by feeding them raw cod or raw salmon. Once tamed, they'll follow you around and will teleport to your side if separated. They'll also sleep when you sleep and will sometimes bring you gifts like rabbit's feet, feathers or raw chicken. Cats scare off creepers and phantoms. They can also see players who have taken a potion of invisibility.

DROPS WHEN DEFEATED

0-2	1-3

SPAWN LOCATION

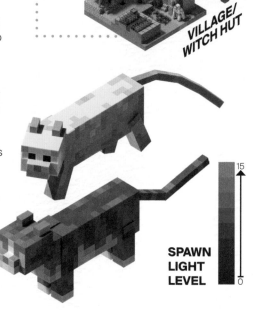

VILLAGE/ WITCH HUT

SPAWN LIGHT LEVEL

15

0

PANDA

BEHAVIOR

Pandas wander around bamboo jungles, searching for bamboo to eat. Some pandas are brown and white instead of black and white. Pandas will follow players within 16 blocks who are holding bamboo. Adult pandas also like to eat cake. If hurt by a player, adult pandas will attack once.

SPECIAL SKILLS

Pandas have different personalities and can be lazy, worried, playful, aggressive or weak. Baby pandas sometimes sneeze, producing a slimeball and making nearby adult pandas jump. Baby pandas can also roll over. Pandas can drop bamboo when defeated.

DROPS WHEN DEFEATED

0-2	1-3

SPAWN LOCATION

BAMBOO JUNGLE

SPAWN LIGHT LEVEL

15

9

0

PARROT

BEHAVIOR

These tameable birds can be found in jungles. There are 5 different colors: red, blue, green, cyan and gray. They can fly a little way above the ground and can also swim. Parrots crowd around other mobs, including hostile mobs.

SPECIAL SKILLS

Parrots can be tamed with seeds and will perch on their player's shoulder. They can also copy the sounds made by other mobs within 20 blocks, e.g. a creeper's hiss. Insert a music disc in a jukebox and nearby parrots will dance. Parrots will die if fed cookies.

DROPS WHEN DEFEATED

1-2   1-3

SPAWN LOCATION

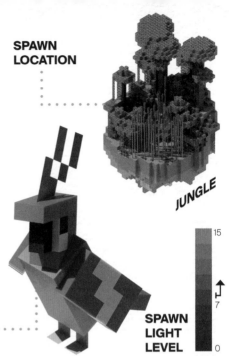

JUNGLE

15

↑
7

SPAWN LIGHT LEVEL

0

TURTLE

SPAWN LOCATION

BEHAVIOR

Turtles can be seen swimming in the ocean, and also found on warm, sandy beaches. They are fast swimmers but move slowly on land. When it's time for turtles to lay their eggs, they always return to their home beach – the beach where they spawned.

WARM BEACH

SPECIAL SKILLS

Turtles follow players if they're holding seagrass. If 2 turtles are fed seagrass, they will breed. They lay 1-4 eggs on their home beach. The eggs take a while to hatch and only hatch at night. When baby turtles become adults, they drop a scute – an item which can be crafted into a turtle shell. This piece of headgear allows players to breathe under-water. Adult turtles can drop seagrass but not scutes.

DROPS WHEN DEFEATED

0-2   1-3

DROPS WHEN ALIVE

1 (BABY)

15

↑
7

SPAWN LIGHT LEVEL

0

FOX

BEHAVIOR

Foxes spawn in groups of 1-3. In regular taiga their fur is red, but in the snowy taiga it's white. They attack chickens, rabbits and baby turtles when on land, and fish if near water. They sleep during the day (unless there's a thunderstorm) and head to nearby villages to scavenge for food at night. They love to eat sweet berries – see page 77 for more berry info.

SPECIAL SKILLS

Foxes can spawn with items in their mouths. They can also pick up dropped items and hold them in their mouth. If you attach a baby fox to a lead and lead it away from its parents, it will trust you and never run away from you.

DROPS WHEN DEFEATED

0-2

SPAWN LOCATION

TAIGA/ SNOWY TAIGA

SPAWN LIGHT LEVEL

15

0

WANDERING TRADER

BEHAVIOR

You'll only ever see 1 wandering trader in your world at any time, and it could be anywhere. They have 2 leashed llamas and will despawn after 40-60 minutes. Sometimes wild llamas form a caravan behind the leashed llamas.

SPAWN LOCATION

SPECIAL SKILLS

Wandering traders offer 1 of 6 random trades when you interact with them. All trades involve emeralds, either as the offered item or as payment. As the sun sets, they drink a potion of invisibility to hide from dangerous mobs. At sunrise they drink milk to remove the effect.

DROPS WHEN DEFEATED

0-2   0-1

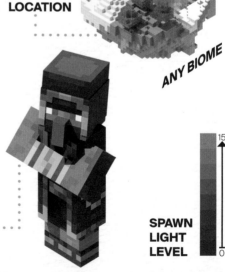

ANY BIOME

SPAWN LIGHT LEVEL

15

0

VILLAGER

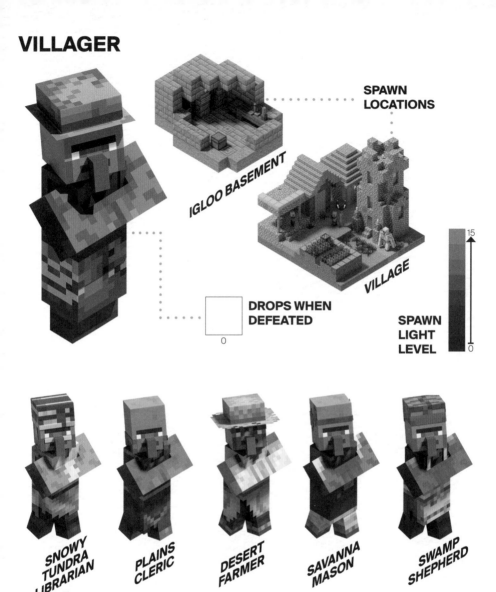

SPAWN LOCATIONS

IGLOO BASEMENT

VILLAGE

DROPS WHEN DEFEATED

0

SPAWN LIGHT LEVEL

15

0

SNOWY TUNDRA LIBRARIAN

PLAINS CLERIC

DESERT FARMER

SAVANNA MASON

SWAMP SHEPHERD

BEHAVIOR

Villagers wander around villages, interacting with each other and performing tasks related to their profession. Each profession has a block related to their job – e.g. a lectern for a librarian, or a stonecutter for a stone mason. Their clothing varies depending on their job and the biome their village is in. You'll also find a villager in every igloo basement.

SPECIAL SKILLS

Villagers like to trade with players – they'll swap a number of useful items for emeralds, and vice versa. Interact with a villager to see what trades they're currently offering. Cartographers will trade explorer maps for emeralds – these rare and valuable maps will lead you to loot-laden woodland mansions and ocean monuments so you can stock up on loot.

NEUTRAL MOBS

 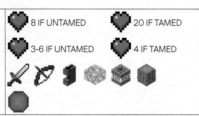

Unfortunately, not all mobs are passive sources of food. A handful of mobs are classified as neutral, which means their behavior varies and they can become hostile under certain circumstances. Keep an eye out for them – they drop some useful items that will aid your progress in different ways.

WOLF

HEALTH POINTS	8 IF UNTAMED	20 IF TAMED
ATTACK STRENGTH	3-6 IF UNTAMED	4 IF TAMED
HOW TO DEFEAT		
ITEMS DROPPED	1-3	

SPAWN LIGHT LEVEL

15
7
0

BEHAVIOR
Wolves roam in packs of 4 and will attack foxes, rabbits, skeletons and sheep on sight. A wolf will become hostile toward any player or mob that attacks them, and any nearby wolves will become hostile, too. Hostile wolves have red eyes and growl.

SPAWN LOCATION

TAIGA

SPECIAL SKILLS
Wolves can be tamed by feeding them bones. Once tamed, they will wear a red collar and follow you around. Tamed wolves can teleport to their owner and will attack any mob that you attack, with the exception of creepers.

ATTACK METHOD
A hostile wolf will pounce on you, inflicting damage with each hit.

POLAR BEAR

HEALTH POINTS	♥ 30
ATTACK STRENGTH	♥ 4-9
HOW TO DEFEAT	🗡 🏹 ▊ ⚒ ◈ ▓
ITEMS DROPPED	🐟 🐟 ⬤

0-2   0-2   1-3

SPAWN
LIGHT
LEVEL

15

7

0

BEHAVIOR
Adult polar bears are neutral but will become hostile if attacked by a player or if they have cubs and a player gets too close to them. Cubs are passive and will run away if attacked, but all the adults within a 41 x 21 x 41 area will become hostile and attack you in retaliation.

SPECIAL SKILLS
Polar bears are fast swimmers. They may drop fish when defeated.

SPAWN LOCATIONS

ICE SPIKES/
SNOWY MOUNTAINS/
SNOWY TUNDRA

ATTACK METHOD
Polar bears will rear up onto their back legs and strike you from above with their front paws.

MOJANG STUFF 🎮
Jeb, lead developer for Minecraft, added polar bears to the game because his wife likes them.

SPIDER

HEALTH POINTS	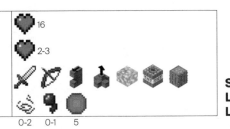 16	
ATTACK STRENGTH	2-3	
HOW TO DEFEAT		
ITEMS DROPPED	0-2 0-1 5	

SPAWN LIGHT LEVEL

15
7
0

BEHAVIOR
Spiders are hostile to players and iron golems if the light level is 11 or lower. If the light level is higher, they won't attack unless provoked. Once hostile, they will continue to pursue you, even if the light level increases.

SPECIAL SKILLS
Spiders can climb over obstacles and up walls. They are immune to poison.

ATTACK METHOD
Spiders will pounce on their opponent, inflicting damage with each hit.

SPAWN LOCATIONS

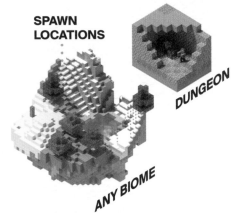

DUNGEON

ANY BIOME

VARIANT: CAVE SPIDER

SPECIAL SKILLS
Cave spiders inflict venom, poisoning you over time. They can fit through spaces that are 1 block wide and half a block tall.

HOW TO DEFEAT	

SPAWN LOCATION . . .

ABANDONED MINE SHAFT

CAVE SPIDER

DID YOU KNOW? ↗
Occasionally a regular spider spawns with a skeleton rider. These horrifying spider jockeys have the speed and agility of a spider combined with the archery skills of a skeleton, making them truly formidable.

ENDERMAN

HEALTH POINTS	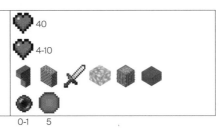	40
ATTACK STRENGTH		4-10
HOW TO DEFEAT		
ITEMS DROPPED		

0-1   5

SPAWN LIGHT LEVEL

BEHAVIOR
Endermen are not hostile toward players unless provoked by attack or by a player looking directly at their head. Once provoked, they will shake and scream, then launch themselves at you to attack. Endermen will also attack endermites on sight.

SPAWN LOCATIONS

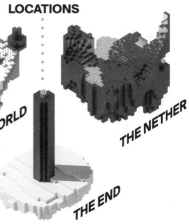

THE OVERWORLD

THE NETHER

THE END

SPECIAL SKILLS
Endermen teleport to avoid danger. They drop ender pearls, which, when thrown, will teleport you. They can also pick up and place certain blocks.

ATTACK METHOD
Endermen will teleport to you and hit you, inflicting damage.

MOJANG STUFF
Endermen hate endermites, so you can use the nasty little bugs as a handy distraction. You can, for instance, put an endermite into a mine cart and set it rolling past endermen, using it to lure them away, or, if you are particularly well prepared, into a pit.

TIP
Wear a carved pumpkin on your head and an enderman will remain neutral even if you look at it. See page 89 to discover how to equip armor.

HOSTILE MOBS

Hostile mobs can make your life incredibly difficult and easily send you back to the respawn screen. They can be particularly dangerous if you encounter them in a small space or while mining underground, but, like neutral mobs, they drop some useful items if you manage to defeat them.

ZOMBIE

HEALTH POINTS		20
ATTACK STRENGTH		2-5
HOW TO DEFEAT		
ITEMS DROPPED		0-2 RARE RARE RARE RARE RARE 0-1 5-12

SPAWN
LIGHT
LEVEL

SPAWN LOCATION

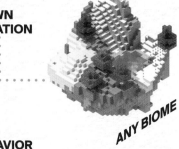

ANY BIOME

BEHAVIOR

Zombies spawn in groups of 4, at light levels of 7 or less. Some zombies spawn wearing armor, which they may then drop upon death. They can't spawn on transparent blocks like glass. They shamble around slowly, with their arms outstretched, making a moaning noise. They catch fire in the sun, so will try to seek shade when the sun rises in the morning.

DID YOU KNOW?

Unlike naturally spawned equipment, zombies never fail to drop the equipment that they have picked up when defeated. Evidence of a guilty conscience, perhaps...

SPECIAL SKILLS

Zombies can break through wooden doors if your difficulty level is set to hard. They can pick up items from the ground, including weapons and tools which they will use, and armor which they will put on. When wearing helmets, zombies are safe from burning in the sun.

USEFUL DROPS

Zombies drop 0-2 pieces of rotten flesh, which you can eat in an emergency but you might get food poisoning as a result. You can also use rotten flesh to breed and heal tamed wolves. Zombies also drop any equipment they have picked up, such as weapons, tools and armor, and will drop their head if killed by a charged creeper's explosion.

ATTACK METHOD

Zombies will pursue players, villagers and iron golems on sight, from 40 blocks away. They aren't a big threat unless you encounter a large group of them – they'll bump into you, inflicting damage and knocking you backward with each hit, potentially into lava or over a cliff.

ZOMBIE VARIANTS

SPAWN LOCATION

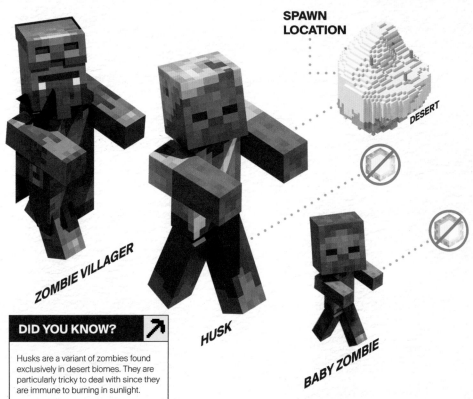

DESERT

ZOMBIE VILLAGER

HUSK

BABY ZOMBIE

DID YOU KNOW?

Husks are a variant of zombies found exclusively in desert biomes. They are particularly tricky to deal with since they are immune to burning in sunlight.

CREEPER

HEALTH POINTS	❤ 20			
ATTACK STRENGTH	❤ 49			
HOW TO DEFEAT	⚔ 🏹 🟫 🟥 🧨 🟦			
ITEMS DROPPED	⚫ ⚫ 🟦 ⚪			
	0-2 0-1 0-1 5			

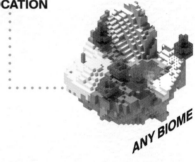

SPAWN LIGHT LEVEL

15
7
0

BEHAVIOR
Creepers move around almost silently, searching for players to target. They have a TNT core that detonates when they are close enough to a player.

SPAWN LOCATION

ANY BIOME

SPECIAL SKILLS
Creepers are immune to burning in sunlight, and continue to creep around in search of players after the sun has risen. They also have the ability to climb up ladders and vines and can do so when pursuing their targets.

ATTACK METHOD
When they're within 3 blocks of a player, creepers will hiss and flash before exploding. Once they begin to hiss, you have 1.5 seconds to get out of the blast radius (7 blocks) if you want to stop the explosion.

USEFUL DROPS

Creepers drop gunpowder, needed to craft TNT, and will drop a music disc if killed by a skeleton's arrow. You'll need a jukebox to play a music disc. Jukeboxes can be crafted from any wood planks.

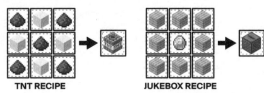

TNT RECIPE

JUKEBOX RECIPE

VARIANT: CHARGED CREEPER

SPAWN LOCATION
When lightning strikes within 3-4 blocks of a regular creeper.

LIGHTNING

ANY BIOME

SPECIAL SKILLS

The charged creeper's explosion is twice as powerful as that of a regular creeper. This explosion will cause any zombies, skeletons or regular creepers unfortunate enough to be in the vicinity to drop their heads. These rare blocks can be used for decoration or worn instead of a helmet. Wearing a mob head will reduce the chance of that mob recognizing you as a player and attacking.

SKELETON

HEALTH POINTS	❤ 20
ATTACK STRENGTH	❤ 1-5
HOW TO DEFEAT	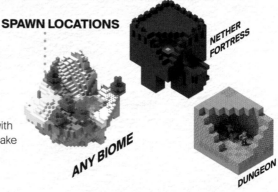
ITEMS DROPPED	0-2 0-2 RARE RARE 0-1 5-8

SPAWN LIGHT LEVEL

15
7
0

BEHAVIOR
Skeletons rattle as they move around, searching for players to attack. They seek out shade at sunrise to avoid burning.

ATTACK METHOD
Skeletons will pursue you on sight. Once they're within 8 blocks, they'll shoot you with arrows, circling you at the same time to make it difficult for you to hit them.

SPAWN LOCATIONS

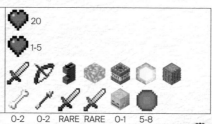

NETHER FORTRESS

ANY BIOME

DUNGEON

SPECIAL SKILLS AND USEFUL DROPS
Skeletons can climb ladders. They can pick up items including tools, weapons and armor, which they will equip/use. They may also spawn wearing armor. Upon death they will drop anything they have picked up, and may drop any naturally spawned equipment.

VARIANT: STRAY
Strays only appear in snowy biomes. They shoot tipped arrows that inflict slowness for 30 seconds. They may also drop 1 tipped arrow upon death.

SPAWN LOCATIONS

ICE SPIKES

SNOWY MOUNTAINS

SNOWY TUNDRA

SKELETON HORSEMAN

HEALTH POINTS	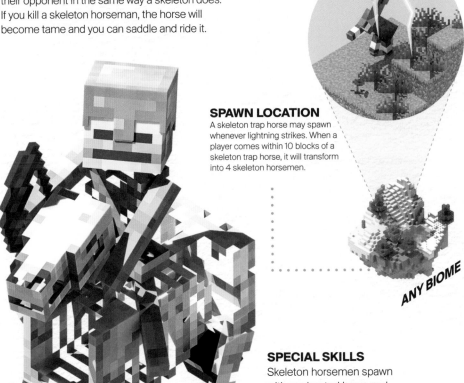 30
ATTACK STRENGTH	1-10
HOW TO DEFEAT	
ITEMS DROPPED	0-2 0-2 5

**SPAWN
LIGHT
LEVEL**

15

10

0

BEHAVIOR
Skeleton horsemen move very fast, and circle
their opponent in the same way a skeleton does.
If you kill a skeleton horseman, the horse will
become tame and you can saddle and ride it.

LIGHTNING

SPAWN LOCATION
A skeleton trap horse may spawn
whenever lightning strikes. When a
player comes within 10 blocks of a
skeleton trap horse, it will transform
into 4 skeleton horsemen.

ANY BIOME

SPECIAL SKILLS
Skeleton horsemen spawn
with enchanted bows and
helmets.

ATTACK METHOD
Skeleton riders attack on
sight, shooting players
with their bows.

55

DROWNED

HEALTH POINTS	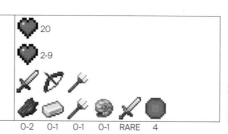 20				
ATTACK STRENGTH	2-9				
HOW TO DEFEAT					
ITEMS DROPPED					
	0-2	0-1	0-1	0-1	RARE 4

SPAWN LIGHT LEVEL

15

7

0

BEHAVIOR

Drowned spawn in oceans and rivers at light levels of 7 or lower. If a zombie drowns, it will become a drowned. They come up onto land at night and are hostile toward players, villagers, wandering traders, iron golems, baby turtles and turtle eggs.

SPAWN LOCATION

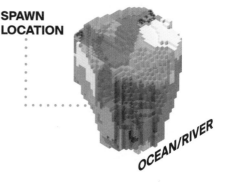

OCEAN/RIVER

ATTACK METHOD

Like zombies, drowned attack with their hands, dealing damage when they touch you. If holding a trident, they will throw it at their target. They will also stamp on turtle eggs in an attempt to destroy them.

SPECIAL SKILLS

Drowned are similar to zombies in many ways, but they can breathe underwater. This makes them even more dangerous - you never know where you might bump into one.

USEFUL DROPS

Drowned may drop their trident, if they have one. Find out more about this weapon on page 91. They may also drop a nautilus shell or a gold ingot.

PHANTOM

HEALTH POINTS	20
ATTACK STRENGTH	4-9
HOW TO DEFEAT	
ITEMS DROPPED	0-1 5

SPAWN
LIGHT
LEVEL

15

7

0

BEHAVIOR

Phantoms only spawn when a player hasn't slept in a bed for 3 in-game days. They appear at night or during thunderstorms in groups of 1-6. Like other undead mobs, they will burn if exposed to sunlight.

ATTACK METHOD

Phantoms can spot players from some distance away. They swoop quickly to attack, hitting their target to deal damage.

SPECIAL SKILLS

Phantoms produce a trail of gray smoke as they move. If they're hit with a splash potion of invisibility, their eyes and smoke trail will still be visible.

SPAWN LOCATION

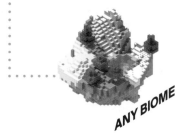

ANY BIOME

USEFUL DROPS

Phantoms may drop a phantom membrane. This strange item can be used to repair elytra – wearable wings that allow you to glide, only found in the End dimension. You can also use a phantom membrane to brew a potion of slow falling. This makes you fall at the same speed as a chicken, which stops you taking damage.

SILVERFISH

HEALTH POINTS	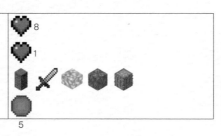	8
ATTACK STRENGTH		1
HOW TO DEFEAT		
ITEMS DROPPED		

5

SPAWN LIGHT LEVEL

15
11
0

BEHAVIOR
When not spawning directly from monster spawners in strongholds, idle silverfish live in monster egg blocks and emerge when a player mines the block.

SPECIAL SKILLS
Silverfish can call other silverfish to their aid when they are being attacked. They can see you through walls and will use this ability to find a path to you.

ATTACK METHOD
Silverfish run toward you and inflict damage, knocking you backward upon contact. You can easily find yourself swarmed.

SPAWN LOCATIONS
Silverfish spawn when monster egg blocks are broken in strongholds, igloo basements and in mountains biomes. They also appear from monster spawners in strongholds.

MOUNTAINS

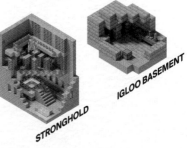

STRONGHOLD

IGLOO BASEMENT

DID YOU KNOW? ↗
If you're quick and defeat a silverfish in a single hit with a diamond sword, nearby silverfish won't be alerted.

ENDERMITE

HEALTH POINTS	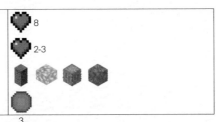 8	
ATTACK STRENGTH	2-3	
HOW TO DEFEAT		
ITEMS DROPPED	3	

SPAWN
LIGHT
LEVEL

15

0

BEHAVIOR
Endermites are the smallest mob. They occasionally spawn when an ender pearl is thrown. They scuttle about, leaving a trail of purple particles behind them, and attack players within 16 blocks. When not attacking players they sometimes try to burrow into blocks.

SPECIAL SKILLS
Endermites will despawn after two minutes. If one endermite is attacked, all nearby endermites will retaliate.

ATTACK METHOD
Endermites run toward you and inflict damage by bumping into you. As with silverfish, you can easily find yourself swarmed.

SPAWN LOCATIONS

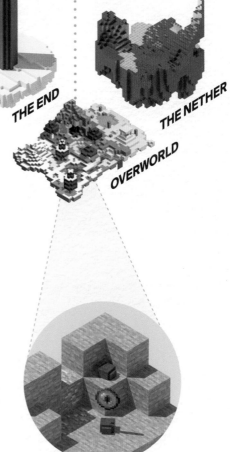

THE END

THE NETHER

OVERWORLD

WITCH

HEALTH POINTS	26						
ATTACK STRENGTH	6-18						
HOW TO DEFEAT							
ITEMS DROPPED	0-2	0-2	0-2	0-2	0-2	0-2	0-2	5

SPAWN LIGHT LEVEL

15
7
0

BEHAVIOR
Witches wander around, searching for players. Their cackle will alert you to their presence.

USEFUL DROPS
Witches may drop up to three different items, from the ITEMS DROPPED list, but no more than two of each unique item.

ATTACK METHOD
Witches throw harmful splash potions (poison, slowness, weakness and harming) at you, while drinking helpful potions to heal themselves.

SPAWN LOCATIONS
Witches can also spawn when lightning strikes within 3-4 blocks of a villager.

ANY BIOME

LIGHTNING

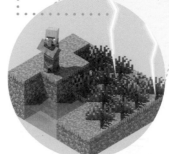

WITCH HUT

DID YOU KNOW?
Witches aren't great at multitasking – they can't attack and drink helpful potions at the same time. Get some hits in when you see them start to heal themselves.

MOJANG STUFF

For a long time, witches had no sound effects. When they were finally implemented, the developers forgot to tell anyone. Players creeping through caves suddenly heard unfamiliar and alarming sounds emanating from the dark. Some were convinced the game was haunted!

SLIME

HEALTH POINTS	 1-16
ATTACK STRENGTH	0-6
HOW TO DEFEAT	
ITEMS DROPPED	0-2 1-4

SPAWN
LIGHT
LEVEL

15

7

0

BEHAVIOR

Slimes come in three sizes: big, small and tiny. They bounce around searching for players to attack and are also hostile toward iron golems.

SPECIAL SKILLS

Slimes can swim in water. They also have the ability to duplicate – if you defeat a big slime, it will split into small slimes, and if you defeat a small slime it will split into tiny slimes. All slimes drop experience points, but tiny slimes also drop slimeballs which can be used in a number of crafting recipes including sticky pistons and leads.

SPAWN LOCATIONS

Slimes spawn below level 40 in all biomes. In swamps they spawn between layers 50 and 70 when the light level is 7 or lower.

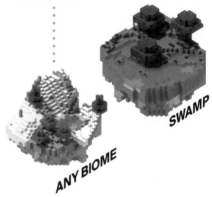

SWAMP

ANY BIOME

ATTACK METHOD

Slimes will bounce into you, inflicting damage when they make contact.

ILLAGER

Illagers look similar to villagers but are dressed in dark robes and their skin has an unhealthy gray hue. There are two variants – the vindicator and the evoker. They can be found in woodland mansions and also spawn as part of raids (attacks on villages triggered by cursed players).

SPAWN LOCATION

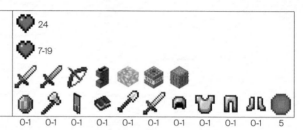

WOODLAND MANSION

DARK FOREST

SPAWN LIGHT LEVEL

15

0

VARIANT: VINDICATOR

HEALTH POINTS	24									
ATTACK STRENGTH	7-19									
HOW TO DEFEAT										
ITEMS DROPPED										
	0-1	0-1	0-1	0-1	0-1	0-1	0-1	0-1	0-1	0-1	5

BEHAVIOR
Vindicators spawn in groups of 2-3. They are hostile toward players and villagers and will pursue them on sight.

ATTACK METHOD
Vindicators will move quickly toward their target, brandishing their axe as a weapon then using it to deal damage.

USEFUL DROPS
Vindicators may drop emeralds when defeated, which can be used to trade with their passive cousins in villages. They may also drop an enchanted book, as well as iron tools and weapons or iron armor.

MOJANG STUFF

The illagers were once called illvillagers and evillagers, but just dropping the "v" was more fun.

VARIANT: EVOKER

HEALTH POINTS	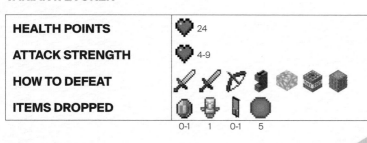 24
ATTACK STRENGTH	4-9
HOW TO DEFEAT	
ITEMS DROPPED	0-1 1 0-1 5

BEHAVIOR
Evokers spawn alone in woodland mansions and as part of raids. They're hostile toward players and villagers.

ATTACK METHOD
The evoker has a special fang attack – it summons a stream of sharp teeth, which rise up out of the floor and bite the evoker's opponent. Evokers can also summon three vexes to join the fight.

USEFUL DROPS
When defeated, evokers drop a rare and powerful item – the totem of undying. When held, this object will prevent the owner from dying.

VEX

HEALTH POINTS	14
ATTACK STRENGTH	5-13
HOW TO KILL	
ITEMS DROPPED	3

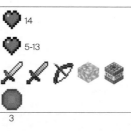

BEHAVIOR
Vexes are summoned by evokers. Armed with swords, they fly at the nearest player or regular villager and attack. They begin to take damage 30-119 seconds after spawning.

SPECIAL SKILLS
Vexes can fly through solid blocks and can often be seen disappearing through the floor.

ATTACK METHOD
Vexes fly at players or villagers and hit them with their sword.

PILLAGER

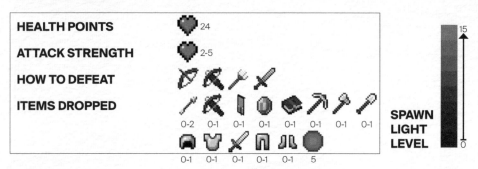

HEALTH POINTS	♥	24
ATTACK STRENGTH	♥	2-5
HOW TO DEFEAT		
ITEMS DROPPED		

0-2 0-1 0-1 0-1 0-1 0-1 0-1 0-1

0-1 0-1 0-1 0-1 0-1 5

SPAWN LIGHT LEVEL

15

0

BEHAVIOR

Pillagers spawn in groups of 2-5, called patrols, 24-48 blocks away from players. They also spawn in and around pillage outposts, and as part of raids (attacks on villages by waves of pillagers, vindicators, evokers, ravagers and witches). Pillagers are hostile toward players, villagers, wandering traders and iron golems.

ATTACK METHOD

Pillagers are armed with crossbows and will shoot their targets. Their crossbows may be enchanted with an effect like multishot (fires 3 arrows at the cost of 1) or quick charge (decreases the crossbow loading time). Pillagers can also ride ravagers.

SPECIAL SKILLS

Each raid has a captain. It could be a pillager, vindicator or evoker, and it will be wearing an ominous banner on its head. If a player defeats the captain, it will drop its banner and the player will be inflicted with the bad omen status effect. If the player then enters a village, this will trigger the start of a raid.

USEFUL DROPS

Pillagers may drop arrows and their crossbow. They can also drop a variety of weapons and armor, as well as emeralds.

SPAWN LOCATION

ANY BIOME

RAVAGER

HEALTH POINTS	 100
ATTACK STRENGTH	7-18
HOW TO DEFEAT	
ITEMS DROPPED	1 20

SPAWN LIGHT LEVEL 15 — 0

BEHAVIOR
Up to 5 ravagers can spawn as part of raids, in or near to villages. Like pillagers, they are hostile toward players, villagers, wandering traders and iron golems. Some ravagers spawn with pillagers or evokers riding them.

SPAWN LOCATION

VILLAGE

ATTACK METHOD
Ravagers use their head to ram their targets, dealing damage and knocking the target backward. Their powerful roar also deals 6 points of damage.

SPECIAL SKILLS
Ravagers can destroy certain blocks by ramming into them – for example, pumpkins, flowers and sugar canes.

USEFUL DROPS
Ravagers drop a saddle when defeated, which can be used to ride horses, donkeys, mules and pigs.

3

SURVIVAL

Now that you're familiar with the Minecraft landscape and its mobs, it's time to start your first game. In this section, you'll learn how to find food and materials to keep yourself safe. You'll discover how to build a shelter and a farm, how to mine for materials and how to defend yourself in combat as you explore.

YOUR FIRST DAY

When you first spawn, it's a race against time to gather resources before night falls and the hostile mobs come looking for you. Every adventure is different, but this step-by-step guide is one option that will keep you safe until day two.

FIRST DAY

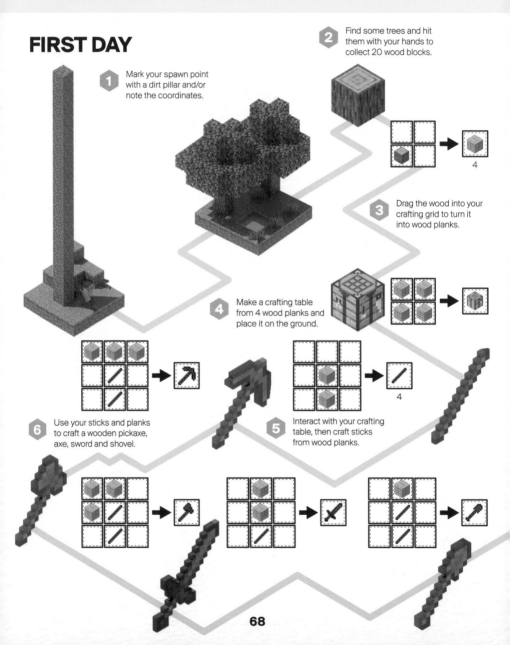

2 Find some trees and hit them with your hands to collect 20 wood blocks.

1 Mark your spawn point with a dirt pillar and/or note the coordinates.

3 Drag the wood into your crafting grid to turn it into wood planks.

4 Make a crafting table from 4 wood planks and place it on the ground.

6 Use your sticks and planks to craft a wooden pickaxe, axe, sword and shovel.

5 Interact with your crafting table, then craft sticks from wood planks.

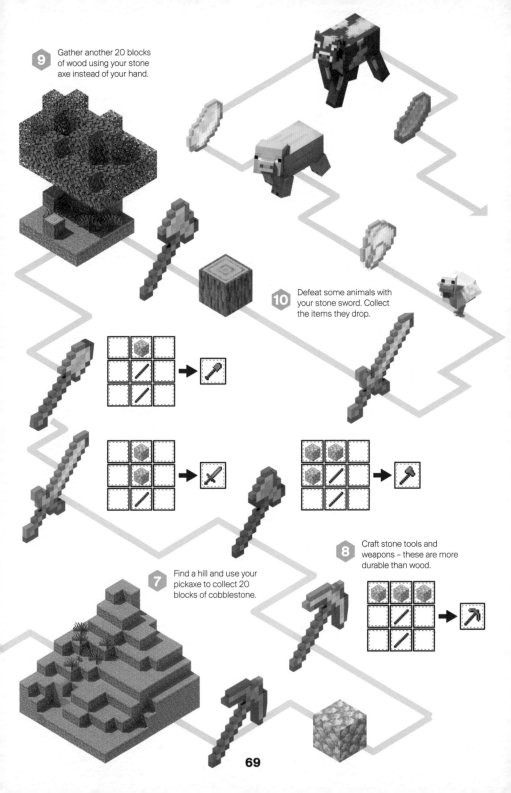

9 Gather another 20 blocks of wood using your stone axe instead of your hand.

10 Defeat some animals with your stone sword. Collect the items they drop.

8 Craft stone tools and weapons – these are more durable than wood.

7 Find a hill and use your pickaxe to collect 20 blocks of cobblestone.

69

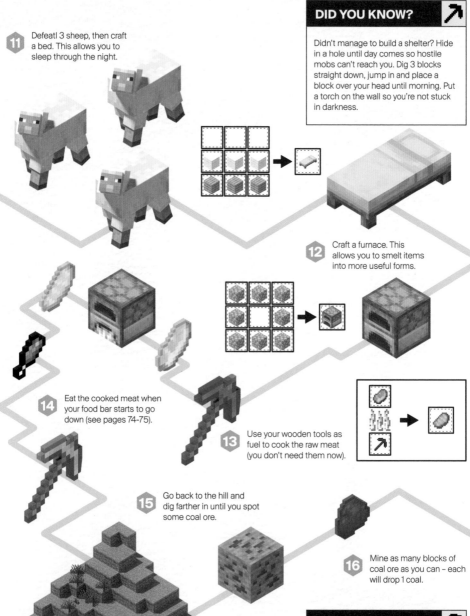

11 Defeatl 3 sheep, then craft a bed. This allows you to sleep through the night.

DID YOU KNOW?

Didn't manage to build a shelter? Hide in a hole until day comes so hostile mobs can't reach you. Dig 3 blocks straight down, jump in and place a block over your head until morning. Put a torch on the wall so you're not stuck in darkness.

12 Craft a furnace. This allows you to smelt items into more useful forms.

14 Eat the cooked meat when your food bar starts to go down (see pages 74-75).

13 Use your wooden tools as fuel to cook the raw meat (you don't need them now).

15 Go back to the hill and dig farther in until you spot some coal ore.

16 Mine as many blocks of coal ore as you can – each will drop 1 coal.

DID YOU KNOW?

No coal ore in sight? Charcoal can be used instead of coal to make torches. Place wood in both furnace slots to create charcoal.

21 Light up your hole using torches to prevent hostile mobs spawning overnight. Shut the door and either sleep in your bed or wait until morning. Hide around the corner, out of sight of the door.

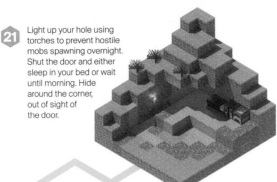

MOJANG STUFF

First day too easy for you? Try something like The 404 Challenge, which became really popular in the early days of Minecraft. The name refers to the world seed number 404, which, at the time, spawned you on a large gravel plane with a huge cave just beneath the surface. You have a day to collect resources above ground, then survive the night inside the cave. The seed no longer works so have fun finding a new one!

DID YOU KNOW?

If you don't manage to make a bed before sunset, use the night to cook any raw food and craft more equipment (see the next page for ideas). You could also start mining beneath your shelter if you're feeling brave...

20 Craft a wooden door and place it on your shelter from the outside.

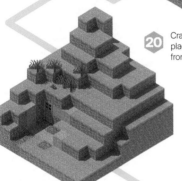

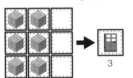

3

19 Expand the hole into an L-shape shelter, so you can hide around the corner.

18 Now you can use coal in your furnace – it'll smelt and cook more items.

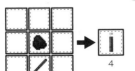

4

17 Craft torches. These can be placed on other blocks to provide light.

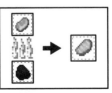

YOUR SECOND DAY

Congratulations – you've made it to day two! Now's the time to fill your inventory with supplies, deal with any resilient hostile mobs that are still lurking and craft more items. Here are some useful crafting recipes to get you started.

CHEST

A chest has 27 slots and is used to store blocks and items. Place two single chests next to each other in your shelter to create a double chest, and transfer materials from your inventory to free up some valuable space.

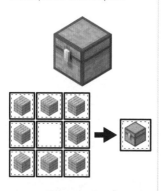

LADDER

Ladders help you ascend and descend quickly and safely. They come in handy when you encounter steep cliffs and when you start mining deeper into the ground. Just place them on the side of the blocks you wish to climb.

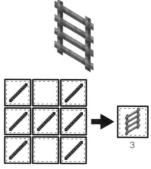

BOAT

Boats allow you to travel across water more quickly – they're a great investment if you live near an ocean and will be essential when the time comes for you to explore new biomes farther from home.

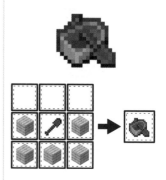

MOJANG STUFF

Pick up a chest and its contents will spill out onto the ground. If you want to carry your stuff around with you, craft a shulker box from shulker shells and a chest.

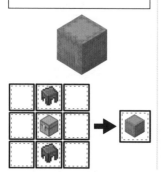

TRAPDOOR

If you start a mine underneath your base, it's a good idea to place a trapdoor on the entrance to prevent hostile mobs from coming up. You'll need to attach the trapdoor to the block by the side of your entrance.

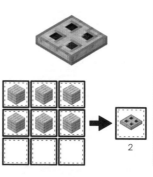

BOWL

You'll need a bowl if you want to cook rabbit stew, mushroom stew or beetroot soup. See pages 76-77 for more information. Bowls can also be used on mooshrooms for instant mushroom stew.

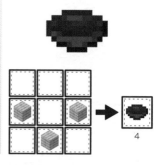

IRON ORE

Your next priority is to find iron ore, which can be smelted into iron ingots and used to make a variety of tools and weapons. Iron ore can be found at sea level and below, in veins of up to 8 blocks. Look for orange flecks among the stone, then mine as many blocks as you can with your stone pickaxe. Once mined, you'll need to smelt iron ore in your furnace to make usable iron ingots, then use it in the crafting recipes below.

IRON TOOLS AND WEAPONS

Upgrade your tools and weapons – use the recipes on page 69 but replace the cobblestone with iron ingots.

IRON ORE

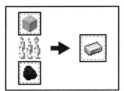

IRON DOOR

Unlike a wooden door, zombies will never be able to break down an iron door. They're more complicated than wooden doors, though, so you'll need to place buttons on the inside and outside to activate them.

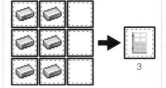

3

FLINT AND STEEL

Flint and steel creates fire when used on top of a solid block. You'll need it to light TNT and activate Nether portals. It's crafted from an iron ingot and flint (sometimes dropped by gravel). See page 53 for the TNT recipe.

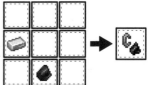

BUCKET

Buckets are tools that allow you to pick up and carry water and lava. You can then place the contents in a new location. Buckets can also be used to milk cows and mooshrooms.

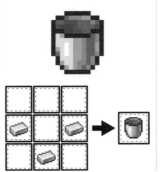

SHEARS

Shears can be used to remove wool from sheep without killing them – and there'll be more of it if you shear rather than kill them. Shears also come in handy when exploring jungle biomes, as they quickly destroy leaves.

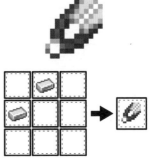

DID YOU KNOW?

You can make gold and diamond tools and weapons – replace the iron ingots with gold ingots or diamonds. Gold equipment wears out quickly but is the easiest to enchant, and diamond equipment is the most durable. See pages 86-87 for tips on how to find gold and diamond.

HEALTH AND FOOD

In Survival mode, you'll need to keep an eye on your health and food bars, which sit just above your hotbar. It's important to eat frequently and heal when you take damage, otherwise your health bar will reach zero and you'll die.

HEALTH POINTS

When you first spawn in Survival mode you'll have a full 20 health points (10 hearts) and a full 20 food points (10 shanks). As you play, you'll take damage, use energy and lose points. To restore your health points, you'll need to eat and avoid taking damage for a while. Your food bar shows you how hungry you are – when it's full you won't be able to eat any more.

You lose health points through:

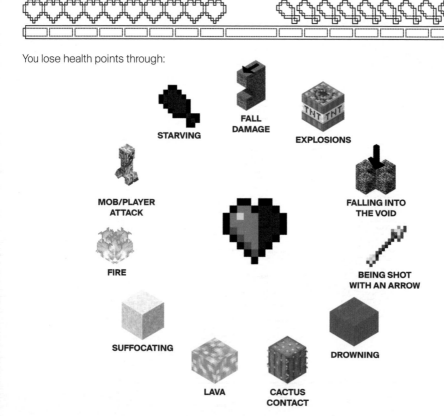

STARVING

FALL DAMAGE

EXPLOSIONS

MOB/PLAYER ATTACK

FALLING INTO THE VOID

FIRE

BEING SHOT WITH AN ARROW

SUFFOCATING

DROWNING

LAVA

CACTUS CONTACT

You lose health points rapidly during combat, so it's a good idea to keep food in a hotbar slot. Different types of food restore different amounts of food points – read on for more details.

RAW BEEF
3 food points

 RAW PORKCHOP
3 food points

 RAW CHICKEN
2 food points

 RAW MUTTON
2 food points

 RAW RABBIT
3 food points

 STEAK
8 food points

 COOKED PORKCHOP
8 food points

 COOKED CHICKEN
6 food points

 COOKED MUTTON
6 food points

 COOKED RABBIT
5 food points

MEAT

Most animals drop raw meat when defeated. This meat will be cooked if they were killed by fire. Meat is an excellent food source as it restores more food points than fruit and vegetables. Cooked meat restores more food points than raw meat.

FISH

If you have a fishing rod and access to water, raw fish are an unlimited resource and an excellent food source. Raw fish can also be obtained by defeating polar bears (see page 47). Cooking fish in a furnace will increase its food points. Use your fishing rod to cast it into the water. When the bobber dips, reel it back in to see what you've caught.

TIP

Fishing doesn't just catch you fish – there's a probability that you'll get junk items and, occasionally, really valuable items like enchanted books. You can put enchantments on your fishing rod, too – that'll increase your chance of snagging the good stuff.

FISHING ROD RECIPE

 TROPICAL FISH
1 food point

 RAW COD
2 food points

 RAW SALMON
2 food points

 COOKED COD
5 food points

 COOKED SALMON
6 food points

FRUIT AND VEGETABLES

Fruit and vegetables don't restore as many food points as meat, but they are a good alternative if you can't find any animals. They are readily available all over the Overworld, if you know where to look, and several can be crafted into more useful items.

DID YOU KNOW?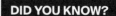

Carrots, potatoes and mushrooms can be crafted into rabbit stew, which restores 10 food points.

 Potatoes can be found in village farms, and zombies occasionally drop potatoes when defeated. A potato can be baked in a furnace to increase its food points.

A potato restores 1 food point, a baked potato restores 5 food points.

 Beetroot can be found in village farms. It can be eaten immediately or crafted into beetroot soup.

Beetroot restores 1 food point, beetroot soup restores 6 food points.

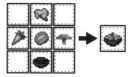

RABBIT STEW RECIPE

BEETROOT SOUP RECIPE

 Carrots can be found in village farms. Zombies occasionally drop carrots when they die.

A carrot restores 3 food points.

 Apples can be obtained by destroying oak and dark oak leaves, and can be found in naturally generated chests. Villagers may also sell apples for emeralds.

An apple restores 4 food points.

 In addition to restoring food points, a golden apple provides an effect known as "absorption I," which absorbs damage for 2 minutes, as well as "regeneration II," which heals damage for 5 seconds. Golden apples can be found in naturally generated chests.

A golden apple restores 4 food points.

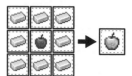

GOLDEN APPLE RECIPE

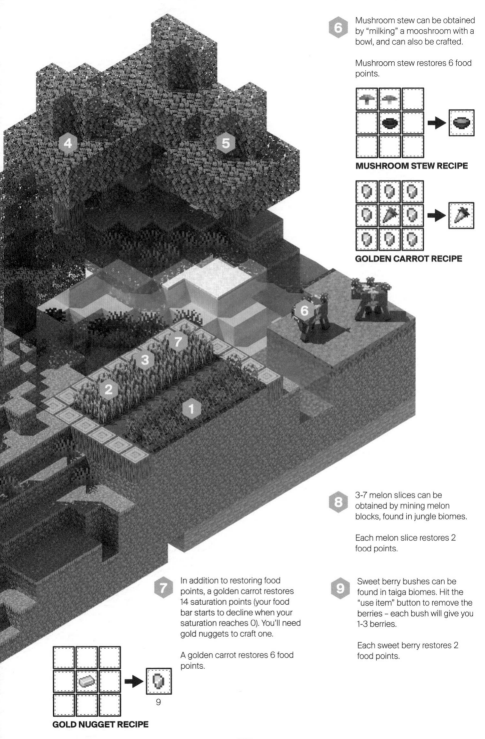

6 Mushroom stew can be obtained by "milking" a mooshroom with a bowl, and can also be crafted.

Mushroom stew restores 6 food points.

MUSHROOM STEW RECIPE

GOLDEN CARROT RECIPE

8 3-7 melon slices can be obtained by mining melon blocks, found in jungle biomes.

Each melon slice restores 2 food points.

7 In addition to restoring food points, a golden carrot restores 14 saturation points (your food bar starts to decline when your saturation reaches 0). You'll need gold nuggets to craft one.

A golden carrot restores 6 food points.

9 Sweet berry bushes can be found in taiga biomes. Hit the "use item" button to remove the berries – each bush will give you 1-3 berries.

Each sweet berry restores 2 food points.

GOLD NUGGET RECIPE

BAKED GOODS

With the right ingredients, you can craft a variety of more complex "baked" goods to top up your food points and add a little variety to your diet. Here's a quick guide to locating and collecting the necessary items.

 Have a look for some wheat in a village farm. You can also hunt for it in loot chests in dungeons, igloos or woodland mansions.

Bread can be found in naturally generated chests. Villager farmers will sell 2-4 breads for an emerald.

Bread restores 5 food points.

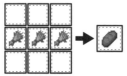

BREAD RECIPE

 Sugar cane is often found near water. Harvest some, then place it in your crafting grid to make sugar.

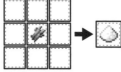

SUGAR RECIPE

BASE INGREDIENTS

  3

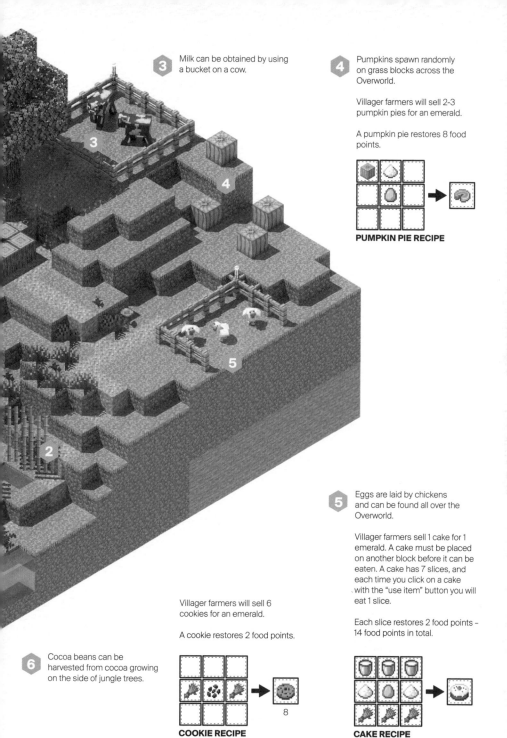

3 Milk can be obtained by using a bucket on a cow.

4 Pumpkins spawn randomly on grass blocks across the Overworld.

Villager farmers will sell 2-3 pumpkin pies for an emerald.

A pumpkin pie restores 8 food points.

PUMPKIN PIE RECIPE

5 Eggs are laid by chickens and can be found all over the Overworld.

Villager farmers sell 1 cake for 1 emerald. A cake must be placed on another block before it can be eaten. A cake has 7 slices, and each time you click on a cake with the "use item" button you will eat 1 slice.

Each slice restores 2 food points – 14 food points in total.

Villager farmers will sell 6 cookies for an emerald.

A cookie restores 2 food points.

8

COOKIE RECIPE

6 Cocoa beans can be harvested from cocoa growing on the side of jungle trees.

CAKE RECIPE

SETTING UP YOUR OWN FARM

Although you can find sources of food throughout the Overworld, life will be a lot easier if you set up a crop and animal farm next to your shelter. That way, you'll have a sustainable source of food right on your doorstep.

BREEDING ANIMALS

As you know, animals have many uses, so an animal farm is a profitable investment. You'll need to stock up on the food each animal responds to, then build a pen and lead them inside to breed.

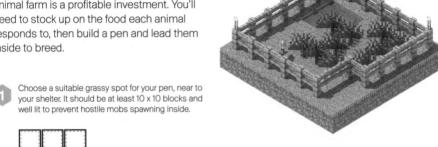

1 Choose a suitable grassy spot for your pen, near to your shelter. It should be at least 10 x 10 blocks and well lit to prevent hostile mobs spawning inside.

WOOD FENCE RECIPE

2 Hunt some animals. If you have string and slime, craft leads so you can easily maneuver the animals into the pen. If not, lead two of each animal into the pen by holding the food item they respond to.

LEAD RECIPE

3 Feed 2 of the same animal when they are within 8 blocks of each other and they will enter love mode. After a moment, a baby animal will appear.

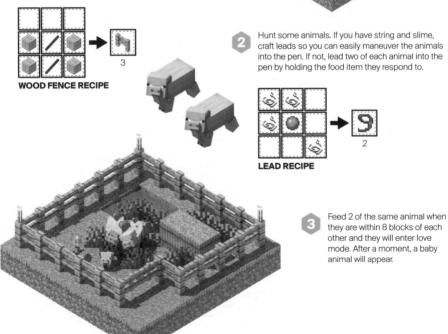

FOODS FOR BREEDING

RABBIT
Dandelions
Carrots
Golden carrots

PIG
Carrots
Potatoes
Beetroot

HORSE
Golden apples
Golden carrots

SHEEP
Wheat

CAT
Raw cod
Raw salmon

COW
Wheat

MOOSHROOM
Wheat

TAMED WOLF
Any raw meat
Any cooked meat
Rotten flesh

LLAMA
Hay bales

CHICKEN
Wheat seeds
Pumpkin seeds
Melon seeds
Beetroot seeds
Nether wart

TIP

Bored of white wool? You can dye your sheep before breeding them to create more colored sheep. The baby sheep will be the color of one of its parents, or it will be a combination, if the colors can mix. Many flowers can be used as dyes, as well as cactus, lapis lazuli, cocoa beans and ink sacs.

CROP FARMING

Different crops require different conditions to grow, and it's important to create the right environment. Choose a flat area of dirt, then follow the steps below to create a crop farm.

CARROTS, POTATOES, BEETROOT AND WHEAT

1 Collect carrots, potatoes, beetroot and wheat from village farms. Wheat seeds can also be collected by destroying tall grass.

2 Craft a hoe – you'll need this to till dirt blocks into farmland.

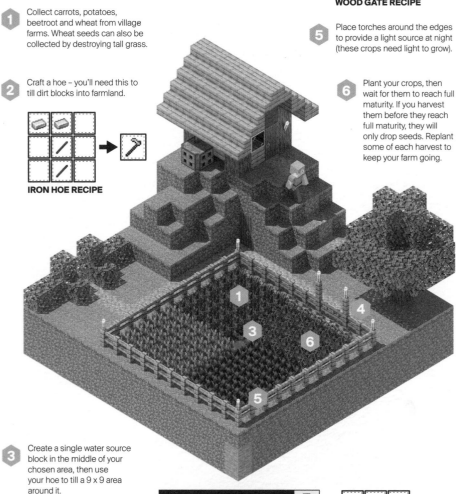

IRON HOE RECIPE

3 Create a single water source block in the middle of your chosen area, then use your hoe to till a 9 x 9 area around it.

4 Surround your farm with fences and a gate to protect it from hungry animals.

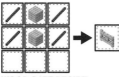

WOOD GATE RECIPE

5 Place torches around the edges to provide a light source at night (these crops need light to grow).

6 Plant your crops, then wait for them to reach full maturity. If you harvest them before they reach full maturity, they will only drop seeds. Replant some of each harvest to keep your farm going.

TIP ↗

Bone meal is a fantastic fertilizer. Use it on your crops to bring them to full maturity immediately.

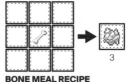

3

BONE MEAL RECIPE

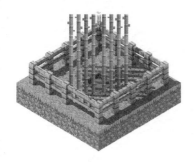

SUGAR CANE

Sugar cane must be planted on dirt, grass or sand that is right next to a water block. It doesn't need light to grow. You'll need sugar cane to make sugar for baking and paper for making books for bookcases. Bookcases will come in useful when you start enchanting items.

> **TIP** ↗
>
> When harvesting fully mature sugar cane (3 blocks high), aim for the middle block so you don't have to replant it.

MELONS AND PUMPKINS

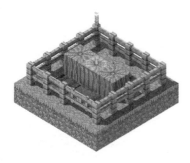

Melons and pumpkins don't need water to grow – just farmland. Till some dirt and make sure there's a block of space to the side, then plant melon or pumpkin seeds. A stem will grow, eventually producing a melon or pumpkin in the adjacent block. When you harvest the melon/pumpkin, the stem will remain and the growth process will begin again.

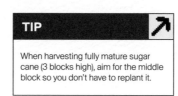

MELON SEEDS RECIPE

PUMPKIN SEEDS RECIPE

Melon seeds can be crafted from melon slices, and can sometimes be found in chests.

Pumpkin seeds can be crafted from a pumpkin, and can sometimes be found in chests.

MUSHROOMS

Mushrooms only grow in areas where the light level is 12 or lower, unless planted on mycelium or podzol (podzol is a type of dirt found exclusively in giant tree taiga biomes). Once planted, mushrooms will spread to nearby blocks that meet their light requirement, as long as there aren't more than 4 mushrooms of that type in a 9 x 9 area.

MYCELIUM   **PODZOL**

83

MINING

Mining is a tricky business, but it's essential if you want to get your hands on rare and useful materials. Many of the rarest items are found beneath the surface of your world, and can only be mined with certain tools.

THE GOLDEN RULES

Follow these golden rules to stay safe as you descend below ground and to ensure you return to the surface laden with the supplies you need.

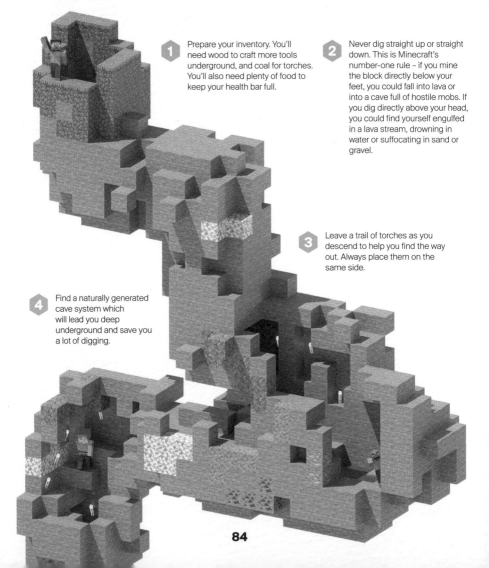

1 Prepare your inventory. You'll need wood to craft more tools underground, and coal for torches. You'll also need plenty of food to keep your health bar full.

2 Never dig straight up or straight down. This is Minecraft's number-one rule – if you mine the block directly below your feet, you could fall into lava or into a cave full of hostile mobs. If you dig directly above your head, you could find yourself engulfed in a lava stream, drowning in water or suffocating in sand or gravel.

3 Leave a trail of torches as you descend to help you find the way out. Always place them on the same side.

4 Find a naturally generated cave system which will lead you deep underground and save you a lot of digging.

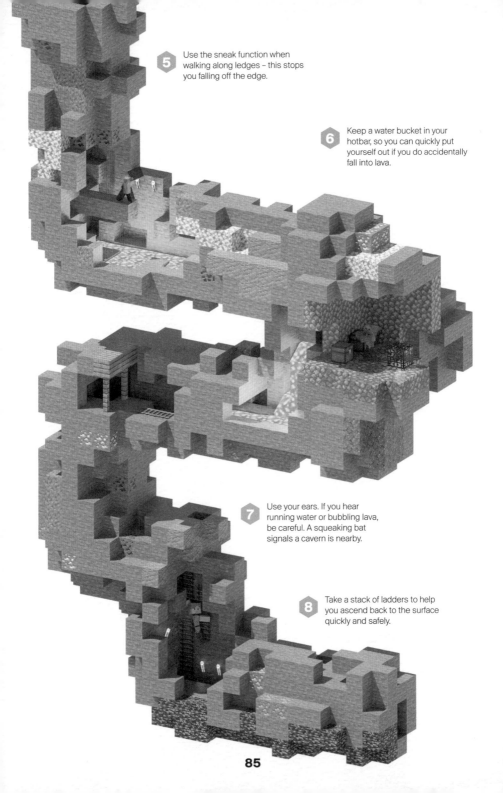

5 Use the sneak function when walking along ledges – this stops you falling off the edge.

6 Keep a water bucket in your hotbar, so you can quickly put yourself out if you do accidentally fall into lava.

7 Use your ears. If you hear running water or bubbling lava, be careful. A squeaking bat signals a cavern is nearby.

8 Take a stack of ladders to help you ascend back to the surface quickly and safely.

MINING FOR ORES

Minecraft's most valuable blocks are found deep underground, near the bottom of the world. Rare ores generate below level 32, where hostile mobs spawn freely in the dark and lava is a serious hazard. You'll need an iron pickaxe or better to mine most ores.

TIP

The best level at which to mine for ores is y=10 to y=15 since all ores generate within this band. Remember to check your coordinates as you descend.

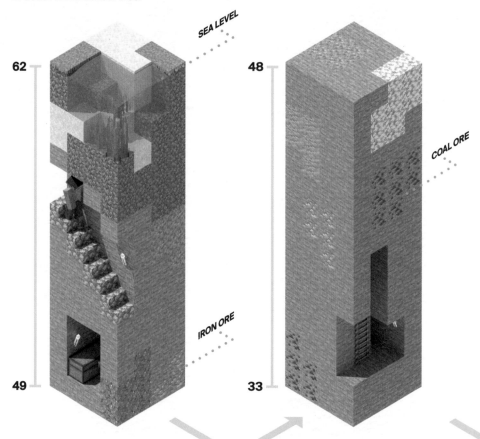

GOLD ORE

Found in veins of 4-8 blocks, at layer 32 and under, gold ore drops itself when mined. You'll need to smelt it in a furnace to turn it into gold ingots. Gold can be used to craft armor, tools and weapons as well as golden apples, clocks and powered rails.

REDSTONE ORE

Redstone ore is found in veins of 4-8 blocks, at layer 16 and under. When mined, each block drops 4-5 redstone. Redstone can be used like a wire to transmit power, and to craft various items, for example, clocks, compasses and powered rails.

LAPIS LAZULI ORE

Lapis lazuli ore is found in veins of 1-10 blocks, at layer 31 and under. When mined with a stone pickaxe or better, each block drops 4-8 pieces of lapis lazuli. Lapis lazuli can be used in enchanting and as a dye.

DIAMOND ORE

Found in veins of 1-10 blocks, at layer 16 and under, each block of diamond ore will drop 1 diamond. Diamonds can be used to craft the most durable tools, weapons and armor, as well as jukeboxes and enchantment tables.

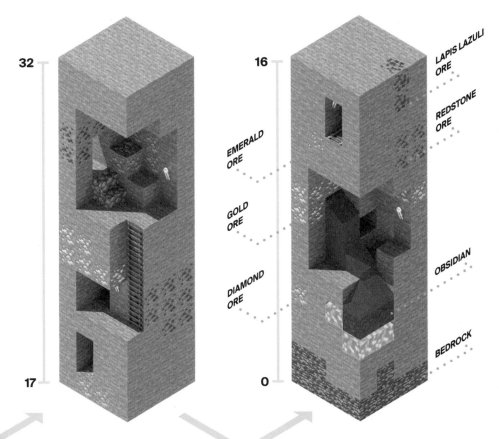

EMERALD ORE

Found in single blocks between layers 4 and 32 in mountain biomes, emerald ore drops 1 emerald when mined. Emeralds can be used in villager trading. See page 45 for more info. They can also be crafted into decorative blocks of emerald.

DID YOU KNOW?

Obsidian is often found toward the bottom of the world where flowing water hits a lava source. It's the toughest mineable block in Survival mode, and is the only block that can be mined only with a diamond pickaxe. You'll need it to make a Nether portal and an enchantment table.

COMBAT

Unless you choose the peaceful option, Survival mode requires you to fight for your life. Pro Minecrafters use potions and enchantments to improve their performance, but here's a guide to basic combat to get you started.

BASIC COMBAT

You'll need a few key items to defend yourself from hostile mobs or enemy players. These crafting recipes will give you a fighting chance.

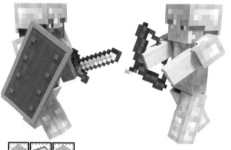

Craft a wood, stone, iron, gold or diamond sword and hit your opponent to inflict damage.

An axe does more damage per hit than a sword, but takes longer to recover.

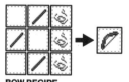

SHIELD RECIPE

A shield allows you to block attacks, reducing the damage you take, but you'll slow to sneaking pace.

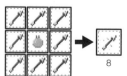

BOW RECIPE

ARROWS RECIPE

4

You can attack hostile mobs or enemy players from a safe distance with a bow and arrows.

8

TIPPED ARROWS RECIPE

Tipped arrows are arrows that have been combined with lingering potions and administer the potion's effect upon contact. You can brew potions, and they are sometimes dropped by witches when they die.

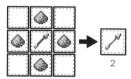

SPECTRAL ARROWS RECIPE

2

Spectral arrows give the glowing effect for 10 seconds, so your target is visible even through solid blocks. Glowstone dust can be found in the Nether and is sometimes dropped by witches.

ARMOR

To help protect yourself from damage, you can craft a full set of armor – a helmet, chestplate, leggings and boots – from 24 units of leather, iron, gold or diamond. Each substance gives you a different level of protection: leather is the weakest, and diamond is the strongest.

DID YOU KNOW?

Equip a carved pumpkin in your helmet slot to wear it on your head. This will come in handy when facing endermen – see page 49 for more details.

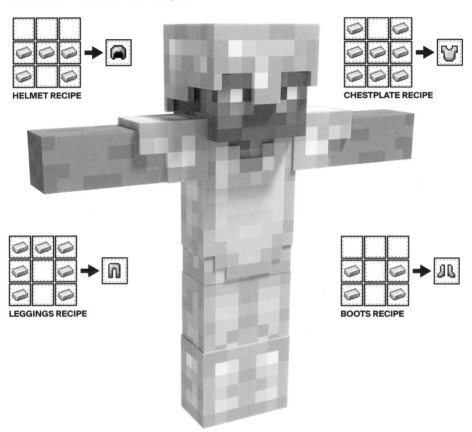

HELMET RECIPE

CHESTPLATE RECIPE

LEGGINGS RECIPE

BOOTS RECIPE

Once you've crafted your armor, open your inventory and locate the four armor slots. Equip your armor here and it will appear on your body, and an armor bar will appear above your health points. Keep an eye on it to check how much durability is left – it will decrease as the armor absorbs damage, and eventually you'll need to craft a new set or repair on an anvil.

ARMOR WILL PROTECT AGAINST:

CROSSBOW

Once you've had some experience with a bow and arrows, you can upgrade to a crossbow. This powerful weapon deals more damage than a bow, and shoots farther. It takes longer to load than a bow and uses arrows or firework rockets as ammunition.

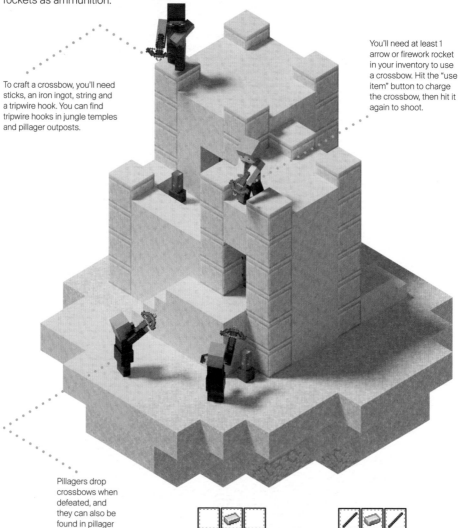

You'll need at least 1 arrow or firework rocket in your inventory to use a crossbow. Hit the "use item" button to charge the crossbow, then hit it again to shoot.

To craft a crossbow, you'll need sticks, an iron ingot, string and a tripwire hook. You can find tripwire hooks in jungle temples and pillager outposts.

Pillagers drop crossbows when defeated, and they can also be found in pillager outpost chests.

TRIPWIRE HOOK RECIPE

2

CROSSBOW RECIPE

TRIDENT

These powerful weapons can be used for melee (hand-to-hand) combat, or for ranged attacks if you throw them at your target.

Hold down the "use item" button for a few seconds to charge your trident, then aim it at your target. When you release the button, the trident will fly toward your target.

If the trident makes contact with a mob or player, it will bounce off them and fall to the ground nearby. If it makes contact with a block, it will become embedded in that block.

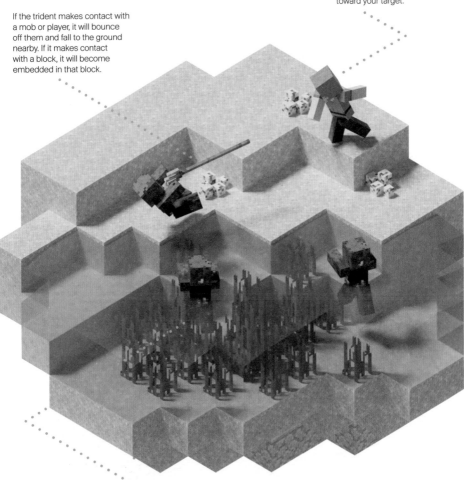

Tridents are rare – drowned mobs may drop them when defeated, but they can't be crafted.

MOJANG STUFF

We recommend enchanting your trident with Loyalty, because it'll come back to you! The higher its level, the faster it'll return.

UPGRADE YOUR SHELTER

So, all that mining and mob combat paid off and your inventory is packed with useful blocks and items just waiting to be used. Now it's time to upgrade your shelter so you have a secure base from which to prepare for your next adventure.

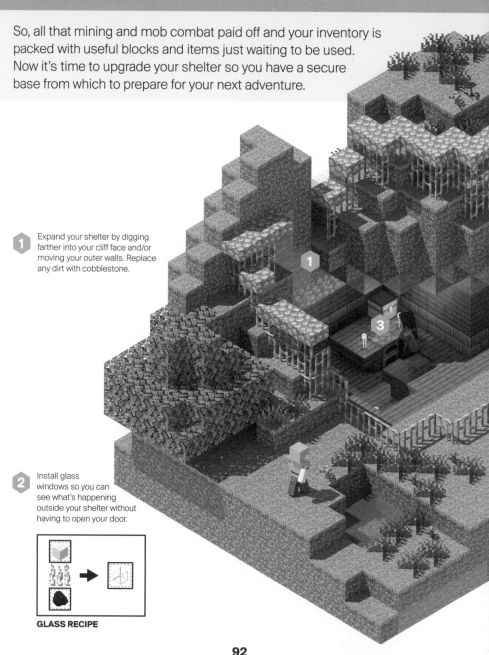

1 Expand your shelter by digging farther into your cliff face and/or moving your outer walls. Replace any dirt with cobblestone.

2 Install glass windows so you can see what's happening outside your shelter without having to open your door.

GLASS RECIPE

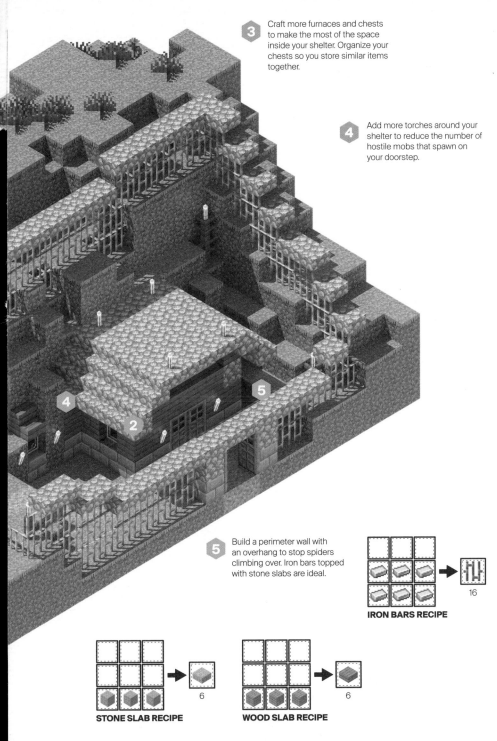

3 Craft more furnaces and chests to make the most of the space inside your shelter. Organize your chests so you store similar items together.

4 Add more torches around your shelter to reduce the number of hostile mobs that spawn on your doorstep.

5 Build a perimeter wall with an overhang to stop spiders climbing over. Iron bars topped with stone slabs are ideal.

16

IRON BARS RECIPE

6

STONE SLAB RECIPE

6

WOOD SLAB RECIPE

NAVIGATING

There's a whole world waiting to be explored beyond the horizon – exciting new biomes full of resources and rare loot, and mobs you've never seen before. It's easy to get lost on long journeys, so make sure you're prepared before you set off.

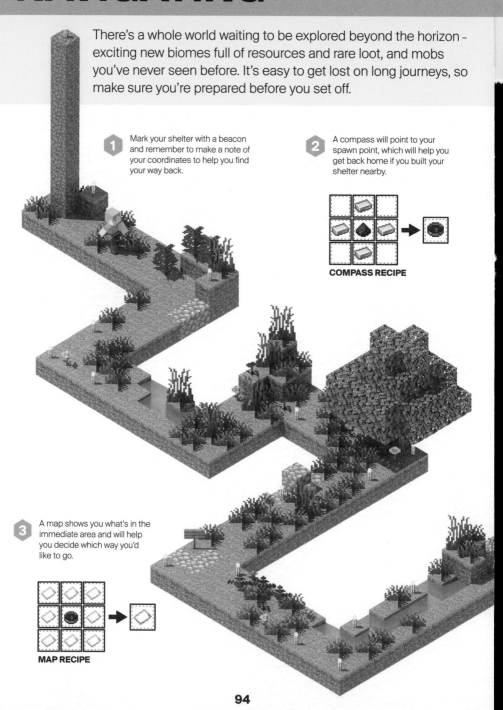

1 Mark your shelter with a beacon and remember to make a note of your coordinates to help you find your way back.

2 A compass will point to your spawn point, which will help you get back home if you built your shelter nearby.

COMPASS RECIPE

3 A map shows you what's in the immediate area and will help you decide which way you'd like to go.

MAP RECIPE

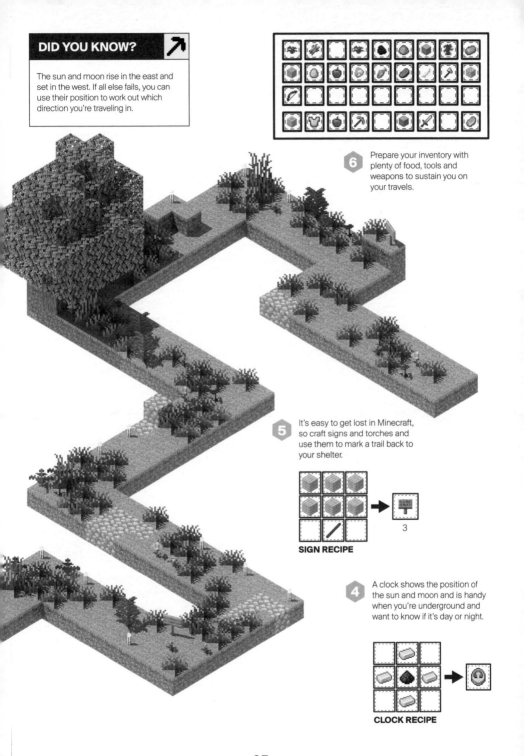

DID YOU KNOW?

The sun and moon rise in the east and set in the west. If all else fails, you can use their position to work out which direction you're traveling in.

6 Prepare your inventory with plenty of food, tools and weapons to sustain you on your travels.

5 It's easy to get lost in Minecraft, so craft signs and torches and use them to mark a trail back to your shelter.

3

SIGN RECIPE

4 A clock shows the position of the sun and moon and is handy when you're underground and want to know if it's day or night.

CLOCK RECIPE

95

STAY IN THE KNOW!

Learn about the latest Minecraft books when you sign up for our newsletter at **ReadMinecraft.com**